Overview Ma

D0942601

Five-Star Trails

The Ozarks

43 Spectacular Hikes in Arkansas and Missouri

JIM WARNOCK

MENASHA RIDGE PRESS

Your Guide to the Outdoors Since 1982

Five-Star Trails: The Ozarks

Cover design: Scott McGrew
Cartography: Scott McGrew, Tim Kissel, and Jim Warnock
Text design: Annie Long
Cover and interior photos: Jim Warnock
Copyeditor: Kerry Smith; proofreader: Laura Franck
Indexer: Rich Carlson

Frontispiece: Elise Falls at Smith Creek Preserve (Hike 12, page 82)

Library of Congress Cataloging-in-Publication Data

Names: Warnock, Jim.
Title: Five-Star Trails : the Ozarks : 40 spectacular hikes in Arkansas and Missouri /
    by Jim Warnock.
Description: [1st Edition] | Birmingham, AL : Menasha Ridge Press, [2016]
Identifiers: LCCN 2016027795| ISBN 9781634040105 (paperback) | ISBN
    9781634040112 (ebook)
Subjects: LCSH: Hiking—Ozark Trail (Mo. and Ark.)—Guidebooks. | Ozark Trail
    (Mo. and Ark.)—Guidebooks.
Classification: LCC GV199.42.O97 W37 2016 | DDC 796.5109778—dc23
LC record available at https://lccn.loc.gov/2016027795

 MENASHA RIDGE PRESS
An imprint of AdventureKEEN
2204 First Ave. S., Ste. 102
Birmingham, AL 35233
800-443-7227, fax 205-326-1012

Visit menasharidge.com for a complete listing of our books and for ordering information. Contact us at our website, at facebook.com/menasharidge, or at twitter.com
/menasharidge with questions or comments. To find out more about who we are and
what we're doing, visit blog.menasharidge.com.

DISCLAIMER This book is meant only as a guide to select trails in and around the
Ozarks in Arkansas and Missouri and does not guarantee hiker safety in any way—
you hike at your own risk. Neither Menasha Ridge Press nor Jim Warnock is liable for
property loss or damage, personal injury, or death that may result from accessing or
hiking the trails described in this guide. Be especially cautious when walking in potentially hazardous terrains with, for example, steep inclines or drop-offs. Do not attempt
to explore terrain that may be beyond your abilities. Please read carefully the introduc-
tion to this book, as well as safety information from other sources. Familiarize yourself
with current weather reports and maps of the area you plan to visit (in addition to the
maps provided in this guidebook). Be aware of park regulations, and always follow
them. While every effort has been made to ensure the accuracy of the information
in this guidebook, land and road conditions, phone numbers and websites, and other
information is subject to change.

Contents

Missouri 148

Appendixes

Dedication

To my wife and family, for patience and a willingness to share me with the trails.

To my hiking friends, fellow educators, and students for inspiring me to take on new challenges.

Acknowledgments

I APPRECIATE THE OUTSTANDING FOLKS I meet on the trails. Special thanks to my circle of hiking friends, from whom I've learned many lessons related to the outdoors and life in general. Thanks also to the volunteers who invest many hours building and maintaining our trails, as well as the professionals who oversee our trails and assist hikers in many ways.

Thanks go to Tim Ernst, whose guidebooks I devoured many years ago while discovering the trails of Arkansas. Later, Tim's photography workshops allowed me to begin packing out visual souvenirs of the beauty I found in the Ozarks.

Thank you to Marla Cantrell, award-winning author and managing editor of *Do South Magazine*, for encouraging me to share my stories and the beauty of the Ozarks.

Thank you to my wife, Becca, for her willingness to walk life's paths with me, regardless of the terrain or weather. I'm also thankful that she realizes I'm a better person if I spend regular time on the trail.

Thank you to my mother, a wonderful writer, for her encouragement and example of lifelong learning. Thank you to my father for taking me hiking and letting me play with his camera when I was young.

—*Jim Warnock*

Preface

FAMILY, FRIENDS, AND HEALTH—FOR ME, Ozark trails connect them all!

When I was 7 years old, my father cleared a narrow path around the back side of our 4 acres in rural south Arkansas. He said it was my trail, not realizing what a special gift this would become. The path was probably no longer than a couple of hundred yards, but to a 7-year-old, it was the perfect launching pad for many adventures on the border of a mixed pine-hardwood forest. My father answered many questions, such as the difference between loblolly and shortleaf pines or why some rocks are sharp edged while others are smooth. Learning these things was important, but the lasting significance came from his time and the interests we shared.

When I was 10, my dad let me play with an old camera from his military days in Korea. I walked freely in the woods, taking pictures of whatever interested me. Sometimes I even put film in the camera. He didn't realize he was planting a seed that would resurface as a passion for photography years later. Sometimes I take that Zeiss Contessa from its shelf and hold the strong metal casing, thankful for this link to memories of my father.

Years later, and farther north, I hiked Ozark trails with my daughters and had the pleasure of watching them discover the beauty of nature. I'm thankful for those family memories that bridge across generations and their connection to the trails.

I've made many friends on the trails and one particular new friend at mile 138 of the Ozark Highlands Trail (OHT) during a thru-hike. She was starving and sick but finished the last 42 miles of the OHT with a friend, Bob, and me, so I took her home. Hiker-dog has been a loyal trail buddy ever since. She's glad I wrote this trail guide because she got to do every trail except the few that don't allow dogs.

For me, hiking was crucial to regaining health and fitness. As a teenager, I had corrective heart surgery and wondered what limitations

A YOUNG HIKER DOES A HANDSTAND ON HAWKSBILL CRAG, WELL AWAY FROM THE EDGE. *(See Hike 11, page 78.)*

I would experience afterward. Years later, I completed three marathons and long-distance backpacking trips, none of which would have happened without the trails and some good medical care. I sent a note to my surgeon thanking him for the good work and letting him know a few of the places that heart he repaired had taken me.

These days, I sometimes say I have an appointment with Dr. Kessler or Dr. Shepherd. My close friends know I'm referring to Kessler Mountain or Shepherd Springs Loop, two trails north of my home in Alma, Arkansas. These fine doctors prescribe a dose of Rock City or a small measure of the Ozark Highlands Trail. I always feel better mentally and physically after a visit, and there are no side effects to these prescriptions, other than the danger of addiction.

Writing this trail guide has been joyful work. Knowing the positive impact that hiking has had on my life, I'm excited to share some of my favorite trails in the Ozarks of Arkansas and Missouri. My hope is that this guide opens doors to wonderful hiking experiences for you, your family, and your friends. I also hope you find some trails that become regular prescriptions for your health and well-being.

—*Jim Warnock*
Blog: ozarkmountainhiker.com

Recommended Hikes

Best for Companion Dogs

Best for Fall Color

Best for Geology

Best for History

Best for Kids

Best for Scenery

Best for Scenery (continued)

Best for Seclusion

Best for Springs and Cascades

CRYSTAL CLEAR WATER FLOWS FROM BLUE SPRING NEXT TO THE CURRENT RIVER. (See Hike 35, page 207.)

EARLY MORNING ON THE SPRINGFIELD CONSERVATION NATURE CENTER LOOP
(See Hike 41, page 236.)

Best for Waterfalls

Best for Wildflowers

Best for Wildlife

Introduction

About This Book

IN THE OZARKS, you'll find a variety of settings, from wilderness hikes to what may feel like a walk in the park. You'll find trails that place you atop high bluffs or ridges and lead you through deep hollows along babbling creeks. These trails will take you across treeless landscapes and through deep-canopied forests.

Ozarks is a broad term for a variety of landscapes found in the northern part of Arkansas and extending into the southern and central part of Missouri. From south to north, the Ozarks include the Boston Mountains, Springfield Plateau, Salem Plateau, and St. Francois Mountains. Technically, the Ozarks extend into Oklahoma, the corner of Kansas, and the edge of Illinois, but for the purposes of this guide, all trails are located within the states of Arkansas and Missouri.

The Ozarks of Arkansas and Missouri have much in common. Taken together, they offer many visual highlights in the south-central United States. A few characteristics unique to Missouri include the large numbers of springs and spring-fed rivers, as well as high mountain glades. The Arkansas Ozarks include many mountain streams and well more than a hundred waterfalls, some very tall. Arkansas also boasts America's first national river, the Buffalo.

Several hikes from the Arkansas River Valley at the extreme southern border of the Ozarks are included, accounting for an additional three Arkansas hikes. The geological plate movements that formed the Ouachita Mountains to the south and the Ozark uplift to the north influenced the formation of the River Valley mountains. What remained following long periods of erosion around the hard cap rocks in the valley were Petit Jean Mountain and Mount Magazine. Hikes on these mountains warrant the attention of a book that

OPPOSITE: SYLAMORE CREEK NORTH OF BLANCHARD SPRINGS CAMPGROUND
(See Hike 20, page 127.)

searches for the area's best hikes. Some may consider it a stretch to include these as "Ozarks hikes," but they are just too good to pass up.

In this guide, you'll find trails of many difficulty levels and a variety of settings, from wilderness to urban. These hikes are classified as day hikes, though some also make excellent shorter backpacking routes. One thing these trails have in common is that I love hiking each and every one of them, and they fall into the four- and five-star rating on one or more criteria.

No hike in this collection merits five stars in all *five* of the rating categories; some, perhaps most, of the hikes will have one, two, three, or four stars in one or more of the rating categories. A hike might merit inclusion in this book because the scenery is spectacular, but it has a two-star rating for trail condition. Another hike with a two-star rating for scenery might have been selected because it's a five-star hike in the category for taking children along.

Narrowing this collection down to 43 was a challenge. Some hikes that I enjoy didn't make the cut, and I've probably not included some hikes that others would have selected. The process is subjective but gives guidance in determining which hike to take based on your needs and situation.

Please contact me through my blog feedback form if you have questions or comments. My goal is to be as accurate as possible. Inevitably conditions and even route changes may occur on some trails. I would appreciate updates as you discover them so that I can post them on my blog for our readers. I welcome trail recommendations too. My black Lab hiking buddy and I are always up for a new trail!

How to Use This Guidebook

THE FOLLOWING INFORMATION walks you through this guidebook's organization to make it easy and convenient for planning great hikes.

Overview Map, Map Key, and Map Legend

The overview map on the inside front cover depicts the location of the primary trailhead for all 43 of the hikes described in this book.

The numbers shown on the overview map pair with the map key on the inside front cover facing page. Each hike's number remains with that hike throughout the book. Thus, if you spot an appealing hiking area on the overview map, you can flip through the book and find those hikes easily by their sequential numbers at the top of each profile page.

Trail Maps

In addition to the overview map on the inside cover, a detailed map of each hike's route appears with its profile. On each of these maps, symbols indicate the trailhead, the complete route, significant features, facilities, and topographic landmarks such as creeks, overlooks, and peaks. A legend identifying the map symbols used throughout the book appears on the inside back cover.

To produce the highly accurate maps in this book, the author used a handheld GPS unit to gather data while hiking each route, and then sent that data to the publisher's expert cartographers. However, your GPS is not really a substitute for sound, sensible navigation that takes into account the conditions that you observe while hiking.

Further, despite the high quality of the maps in this guidebook, the publisher and author strongly recommend that you always carry an additional map, such as the ones noted in each entry opener's listing for "Maps."

Elevation Profile

The elevation profile represents the rises and falls of the trail as viewed from the side, over the complete distance (in miles) of that trail. On the diagram's vertical axis, or height scale, the number of feet indicated between each tick mark lets you visualize the climb. To avoid making flat hikes look steep and steep hikes appear flat, varying height scales provide an accurate image of each hike's climbing challenge. For example, one hike's scale might rise to 3,000 feet, while another goes to 600 feet.

Also, each entry's opener will list the elevation at the hike *trailhead*, and it will list the elevation *peak*.

The Hike Profile

Each hike profile opens with the hike's star ratings, GPS trailhead coordinates, and other key at-a-glance information—from the trail's distance and configuration, to contacts for local information. Each profile also includes a map (see "Trail Maps," page 3). The main text for each profile includes four sections: "Overview," "Route Details," "Nearby Attractions," and "Directions" (for driving to the trailhead area).

STAR RATINGS

The hikes in *Five-Star Trails: The Ozarks* were carefully chosen to give the hiker an overall five-star experience and represent the diversity of trails found in the region. Each hike was assigned a one- to five-star rating in each of the following categories: scenery, trail condition, suitability for children, level of difficulty, and degree of solitude. While one hike may merit five stars for its stunning scenery, that same trail may rank as a two-star trail for children. Similarly, another hike might receive two stars for difficulty but earn five stars for solitude. It's rare that any trail receives five stars in all five categories; nevertheless, each trail offers excellence in at least one category, if not others. Here's how the star ratings for each of the five categories break down:

FOR SCENERY:

★ ★ ★ ★ ★ Unique, picturesque panoramas

★ ★ ★ ★ Diverse vistas

★ ★ ★ Pleasant views

★ ★ Unchanging landscape

★ Not selected for scenery

FOR TRAIL CONDITION:

★ ★ ★ ★ ★ Consistently well maintained

★ ★ ★ ★ Stable, with no surprises

★ ★ ★ Average terrain to negotiate

★ ★ Inconsistent, with good and poor areas

★ Rocky, overgrown, or often muddy

FOR CHILDREN:

★ ★ ★ ★ ★   Babies in strollers are welcome

★ ★ ★ ★   Fun for anyone past the toddler stage

★ ★ ★   Good for young hikers with proven stamina

★ ★   Not enjoyable for children

★   Not advisable for children

FOR DIFFICULTY:

★ ★ ★ ★ ★   Grueling

★ ★ ★ ★   Strenuous

★ ★ ★   Moderate: won't beat you up—but you'll know you've been hiking

★ ★   Easy with patches of moderate

★   Good for a relaxing stroll

FOR SOLITUDE:

★ ★ ★ ★ ★   Positively tranquil

★ ★ ★ ★   Spurts of isolation

★ ★ ★   Moderately secluded

★ ★   Crowded on weekends and holidays

★   Steady stream of individuals and/or groups

GPS TRAILHEAD COORDINATES

As noted in "Trail Maps" on page 3, the author used a handheld GPS unit to obtain geographic data and sent the information to the publisher's cartographers. In the opener for each hike profile, the coordinates—the intersection of the latitude (north) and longitude (west)—will orient you from the trailhead. In some cases, you can drive within viewing distance of a trailhead. Other hiking routes require a short walk to the trailhead from a parking area.

You will also note that this guidebook uses the **degree–decimal minute format** for presenting the latitude and longitude GPS coordinates.

> **DEGREE–DECIMAL MINUTE FORMAT**
> **N37° 39.186' W90° 41.335'**

The latitude and longitude grid system is likely quite familiar to you, but here is a refresher, pertinent to visualizing the GPS coordinates:

Imaginary lines of latitude—called parallels and approximately 69 miles apart from each other—run horizontally around the globe. The equator is established to be 0°, and each parallel is indicated by degrees from the equator: up to 90°N at the North Pole, and down to 90°S at the South Pole.

Imaginary lines of longitude—called meridians—run perpendicular to latitude lines. Longitude lines are likewise indicated by degrees. Starting from 0° at the Prime Meridian in Greenwich, England, they continue to the east and west until they meet 180° later at the International Date Line in the Pacific Ocean. At the equator, longitude lines also are approximately 69 miles apart, but that distance narrows as the meridians converge toward the North and South Poles.

To convert GPS coordinates given in degrees, minutes, and seconds to the format shown above in degrees–decimal minutes, the seconds are divided by 60. For more on GPS technology, visit usgs.gov.

DISTANCE AND CONFIGURATION

Distance notes the length of the hike round-trip, from start to finish. If the hike description includes options to shorten or extend the hike, those round-trip distances will also be factored here. Configuration defines the trail as a loop, an out-and-back (taking you in and out via the same route), a figure eight, or a balloon.

HIKING TIME

Two miles per hour is a general rule of thumb for the hiking times noted in this guidebook. That pace typically allows time for taking photos and admiring views. If you spend extended time with photography or exploring a waterfall, your hiking pace will be slower, even approaching 1 mile per hour. When deciding whether or not to follow a particular trail in this guidebook, consider your own pace, the weather, your general physical condition, and your energy level that day.

HIGHLIGHTS

Waterfalls, historic sites, or other features that draw hikers to this trail are emphasized here.

ELEVATION

In each trail's opener, you will see the elevation (in feet) at the trail-head and another figure for the peak height on that route. The full hike profile also includes a complete elevation profile (see page 3).

ACCESS

Fees or permits required to hike the trail are detailed here—and noted if there are none. Trail-access hours are also shown here.

MAPS

Resources for maps, in addition to those in this guidebook, are listed here. As previously noted, the publisher and author recommend that you carry more than one map—and that you consult those maps before heading out on the trail in order to resolve any confusion or discrepancy. All USGS maps recommended in this guide are 7.5-minute.

FACILITIES

This item alerts you to restrooms, phones, water, picnic tables, and other basics at or near the trailhead.

WHEELCHAIR ACCESS

At a glance, you'll see if there are paved sections or other areas for safely using a wheelchair.

COMMENTS

Here you will find assorted nuggets of information, such as whether or not dogs are allowed on the trails.

CONTACTS

Listed here are phone numbers and website addresses for checking trail conditions and gleaning other day-to-day information.

Overview, Route Details, Nearby Attractions, and Directions

These four elements provide the main text about the hike. "Overview" gives you a quick summary of what to expect on that trail; the

"Route Details" guide you on the hike, start to finish; "Nearby Attractions" suggests appealing area sites, such as restaurants, museums, and other trails. "Directions" will get you to the trailhead from a well-known road or highway.

Weather

THE OZARKS HAVE A YEAR-ROUND HIKING SEASON, with the possible exception of the hottest part of the summer, when bugs are out and creeks are dry. Fall, a favorite hiking season, tends to define the beginning of the Ozark hiking year. Colorful foliage and cooler, yet unpredictable, temperatures characterize fall. You might experience cold snaps and sometimes unexpectedly warm temperatures. Fall is usually a dry season in the Ozarks, but this, too, is not a hard-and-fast rule. Winter is a great season, with more solitude, open views due to the trees being leafless, and, best of all, no bugs. Drawbacks to winter include the possibility of bitterly cold temperatures and unpredictable road conditions. Snow-covered roads rarely last more than a few days, though melt off can be slow on shaded forest roads. Springtime is a popular season, with milder temperatures, colorful wildflowers, and the possibility of picturesque waterfalls and cascades. With those water features comes the possibility of flash flooding and dangerous creek crossings. Summer, with stunning wildflower displays, is still a possible season for hiking, but you might consider higher elevations in the Ozarks and target the occasional cool snaps.

The tables on the facing page list average temperatures and precipitation by month for the Fayetteville, Arkansas, and Springfield, Missouri, regions. For each month, "Hi Temp" is the average daytime high; "Lo Temp" is the average nighttime low; and "Rain" is the average precipitation, followed by "Snow" for average snowfall.

★ FAYETTEVILLE, ARKANSAS ★

MONTH	HI TEMP	LO TEMP	RAIN	SNOW
January	46° F	26° F	2.6"	2"
February	51° F	30° F	2.4"	2"
March	59° F	38° F	4.0"	0"
April	69° F	47° F	4.3"	0"
May	76° F	56° F	5.2"	0"
June	84° F	65° F	4.8"	0"
July	89° F	69° F	3.2"	0"
August	89° F	68° F	3.0"	0"
September	81° F	59° F	4.6"	0"
October	70° F	47° F	4.1"	0"
November	59° F	38° F	4.3"	0"
December	48° F	29° F	3.0"	1"

★ SPRINGFIELD, MISSOURI ★

MONTH	HI TEMP	LO TEMP	RAIN	SNOW
January	43° F	22° F	2.5"	5"
February	48° F	26° F	2.5"	4"
March	58° F	35° F	3.6"	2"
April	67° F	44° F	4.3"	0"
May	75° F	54° F	5.1"	0"
June	84° F	63° F	4.8"	0"
July	89° F	68° F	3.7"	0"
August	89° F	67° F	3.5"	0"
September	80° F	58° F	4.6"	0"
October	69° F	47° F	3.6"	0"
November	57° F	35° F	4.2"	1"
December	45° F	25° F	3.0"	5"

Water

HOW MUCH IS ENOUGH? Well, one simple physiological fact should convince you to err on the side of excess when deciding how much water to pack: a hiker walking steadily in 90°F heat needs approximately 10 quarts of fluid per day. That's 2.5 gallons. A good rule of thumb is to hydrate prior to your hike, carry (and drink) 6 ounces of water for every mile you plan to hike, and hydrate again after the hike. For most people, the pleasures of hiking make carrying water a relatively minor price to pay to remain safe and healthy. So pack more water than you anticipate needing even for short hikes.

If you are tempted to drink "found" water, do so with extreme caution. Many ponds and lakes encountered by hikers are fairly stagnant, and the water tastes terrible. Drinking such water presents inherent risks for thirsty trekkers. Giardia parasites contaminate many water sources and cause the dreaded intestinal giardiasis that can last for weeks after ingestion. For information, visit the Centers for Disease Control website at cdc.gov/parasites/giardia.

In any case, effective treatment is essential before using any water source found along the trail. Boiling water for 2–3 minutes is always a safe measure for camping, but day hikers can consider iodine tablets, approved chemical mixes, filtration units rated for giardia, and ultraviolet filtration. Some of these methods (for example, filtration with an added carbon filter) remove bad tastes typical in stagnant water, while others add their own taste. As a precaution, carry a means of water purification to help in a pinch if you realize you have underestimated your consumption needs.

Clothing

WEATHER, UNEXPECTED TRAIL CONDITIONS, fatigue, extended hiking duration, and wrong turns can individually or collectively turn a great outing into a very uncomfortable one at best—and a life-threatening one at worst. Thus, proper attire plays a key role in staying comfortable and, sometimes, in staying alive. Here are some helpful guidelines:

★ Choose silk, wool, or synthetics for maximum comfort in all of your hiking attire—from hats to socks and in between. Cotton is fine if the weather remains dry and stable, but you won't be happy if that material gets wet.

★ Always wear a hat, or at least tuck one into your day pack or hitch it to your belt. Hats offer all-weather sun and wind protection as well as warmth if it turns cold.

★ Be ready to layer up or down as the day progresses and the mercury rises or falls. Today's outdoor wear makes layering easy, with such designs as jackets that convert to vests and zip-off or button-up legs.

★ Wear hiking boots or sturdy trail running shoes with toe protection. Flip-flopping along a paved urban greenway is one thing, but never hike a trail in open sandals or casual sneakers. Your bones and arches need support, and your skin needs protection.

★ Pair that footwear with good wool-blend socks. If you prefer not to sheathe your feet when wearing hiking sandals, tuck the socks into your day pack; you may need them if the weather plummets or if you hit rocky turf and pebbles begin to irritate your feet. And, in an emergency, if you have lost your gloves, you can adapt the socks into mittens.

★ Don't leave rainwear behind, even if the day dawns clear and sunny. Weather in the Ozarks can change quickly. Tuck into your day pack, or tie around your waist, a jacket that is breathable and either water resistant or waterproof. Investigate different choices at your local outdoors retailer. If you are a frequent hiker, ideally you'll have more than one rainwear weight, material, and style in your closet to protect you in all seasons in your regional climate and hiking microclimates.

Essential Gear

TODAY YOU CAN BUY OUTDOOR VESTS that have up to 20 pockets shaped and sized to carry everything from toothpicks to binoculars. Or, if you don't aspire to feel like a burro, you can neatly stow all of these items in your day pack or backpack. The following list showcases never-hike-without-them items. They are listed in alphabetical order, as all are important:

★ Extra clothes (raingear, warm hat, gloves, and change of socks and shirt)

★ Extra food (trail mix, granola bars, or other high-energy foods)

★ Flashlight or headlamp with extra bulb and batteries

★ Insect repellent (For some areas and seasons, this is extremely vital.)

★ Maps and a high-quality compass (Even if you know the terrain from previous hikes, don't leave home without these tools. And, as previously noted, bring maps in addition to those in this guidebook, and consult your maps prior to the hike. If you are versed in GPS usage, bring that device too; but don't rely on it as your sole navigational tool, as battery life can dwindle or die, and be sure to compare its guidance with that of your maps.)

★ Medications you routinely need available

★ Pocketknife and/or multitool

★ Sunscreen (Note the expiration date on the tube or bottle; it's usually embossed on the top.)

★ Water (As emphasized more than once in this book, bring more than you think you will drink. Depending on your destination, you may want to bring a container and iodine or a filter for purifying water in case you run out.)

★ Whistle (This little gadget will be your best friend in an emergency.)

★ Windproof matches and/or a lighter, as well as a fire starter

First Aid Kit

IN ADDITION TO THE ITEMS ABOVE, those below may appear overwhelming for a day hike. But any paramedic will tell you that the products listed here—in alphabetical order, because all are important—are just the basics. The reality of hiking is that you can be out for a week of backpacking and acquire only a mosquito bite. Or you can hike for an hour, slip, and suffer a bleeding abrasion or broken bone. Fortunately, these listed items will collapse into a very small space. You also may purchase convenient, prepackaged kits at your pharmacy or online.

★ Ace bandages or Spenco joint wraps

★ Adhesive bandages

★ Antibiotic ointment (Neosporin or the generic equivalent)

★ Athletic tape

★ Benadryl or the generic equivalent diphenhydramine (in case of allergic reactions)

★ Blister kit (such as Moleskin/Spenco Second Skin)

★ Butterfly-closure bandages

★ Epinephrine in a prefilled syringe (typically by prescription only, and for people known to have severe allergic reactions)

★ Gauze (one roll and a half dozen 4-by-4-inch pads)

★ Hydrogen peroxide or iodine

★ Ibuprofen or acetaminophen

Note: Consider your intended terrain and the number of hikers in your party before you exclude any article cited above. A botanical garden stroll may not inspire you to carry a complete kit, but anything beyond that warrants precaution. When hiking alone, you should always be prepared for a medical need. And if you are a twosome or with a group, one or more people in your party should be equipped with first aid material.

General Safety

THE FOLLOWING TIPS may have the familiar ring of your mother's voice as you take note of them.

★ **ALWAYS LET SOMEONE KNOW WHERE YOU WILL BE HIKING AND HOW LONG YOU EXPECT TO BE GONE.** It's a good idea to give that person a copy of your route, particularly if you are headed into any isolated area. Let him or her know when you return.

★ **ALWAYS SIGN IN AND OUT OF ANY TRAIL REGISTERS PROVIDED.** Don't hesitate to comment on the trail condition if space is provided; that's your opportunity to alert others to any problems you encounter.

★ **DO NOT COUNT ON A CELL PHONE FOR YOUR SAFETY.** Reception may be spotty or nonexistent on the trail, even on an urban walk—especially if it is embraced by towering trees.

★ **ALWAYS CARRY FOOD AND WATER,** even for a short hike. And bring more water than you think you will need.

★ **ASK QUESTIONS.** State forest and park employees are there to help. It's much easier to solicit advice before a problem occurs, and it will help you avoid a mishap away from civilization when it's too late to amend an error.

★ **STAY ON DESIGNATED TRAILS.** Even on the most clearly marked trails, there is usually a point where you have to stop and consider which direction to head. If you become disoriented, don't panic. As soon as you think you may be off track, stop, assess your current direction, and then retrace your steps to the point where you went astray. Using a map, a compass, and this book, and keeping in mind what you have passed thus far, reorient yourself, and trust your judgment on which way to continue. If you become absolutely unsure of how to continue, return to your vehicle the way you came in. Should you become completely lost and have no idea how to find the trailhead, remaining in place along the trail and waiting for help is most often the best option for adults and always the best option for children.

★ **ALWAYS CARRY A WHISTLE.** It may be a lifesaver if you get lost or hurt.

★ **BE ESPECIALLY CAREFUL WHEN CROSSING STREAMS.** Whether you are fording the stream or crossing on a log, make every step count. If you have any doubt about maintaining your balance on a log, ford the stream instead: use a trekking pole or stout stick for balance *and face upstream as you cross.* If a stream seems too deep to ford, turn back. Whatever is on the other side is not worth risking your life.

★ **BE CAREFUL AT OVERLOOKS.** While these areas may provide spectacular views, they are potentially hazardous. Stay back from the edge of outcrops, and make absolutely sure of your footing; a misstep can mean a nasty and possibly fatal fall.

★ **STANDING DEAD TREES** and storm-damaged living trees pose a significant hazard to hikers. These trees may have loose or broken limbs that could fall at any time. While walking beneath trees, and when choosing a spot to rest or enjoy your snack, look up.

★ **KNOW THE SYMPTOMS OF SUBNORMAL BODY TEMPERATURE, OR HYPOTHERMIA.** Shivering and forgetfulness are the two most common indicators of this stealthy killer. Hypothermia can occur at any elevation, even in the summer, especially when the hiker is wearing lightweight cotton clothing. If symptoms develop, get to shelter, hot liquids, and dry clothes as soon as possible.

★ **LIKEWISE, KNOW THE SYMPTOMS OF HEAT EXHAUSTION, OR HYPER-THERMIA.** Light-headedness and loss of energy are the first two indicators. If you feel these symptoms, find some shade, drink your water, remove as many layers of clothing as practical, and stay put until you cool down. Marching through heat exhaustion leads to heatstroke—which can be fatal. Dilated pupils; dry, hot, flushed skin; a rapid pulse; high fever; and abnormal breathing are all symptoms of heatstroke. If you should be sweating and you're not, that's the signature warning sign. Your hike is over at that point—heatstroke is a life-threatening condition that can cause seizures, convulsions, and eventually death. If you or a companion reaches that point, do whatever you can to cool down and find help immediately.

★ **TAKE ALONG YOUR BRAIN.** A cool, calculating mind is the single most important asset on the trail. It allows you to think before you act. Plan ahead. Watch your step. Avoid accidents before they happen. Enjoy a rewarding and relaxing hike.

Animal, Insect, and Plant Hazards

BELOW IS ADVICE ON DEALING WITH VARIOUS HAZARDS that might be encountered when hiking in the Ozarks. These hazards are listed in the order that they are likely to occur.

Ticks

Ticks are often found on brush and tall grass, where they seem to be waiting to hitch a ride on a warm-blooded passerby. Adult ticks are most active April into May and again October into November. Among the varieties of ticks, the black-legged tick, commonly called the deer tick, is the primary carrier of Lyme disease. Wear light-colored clothing, making it easier for you to spot ticks before they migrate to your skin. At the end of the hike, visually check your hair, back of neck, armpits, and socks. During your posthike shower, take a moment to do a more complete body check. For ticks that are already embedded, removal with tweezers is best. Use disinfectant solution on the wound.

Poison Ivy, Oak, and Sumac

Recognizing and avoiding poison ivy, oak, and sumac are the most effective ways to prevent the painful, itchy rashes associated with these plants. Poison ivy occurs as a vine or ground cover, three leaf-lets to a leaf; poison oak occurs as either a vine or shrub, also with three leaflets; and poison sumac flourishes in swampland, each leaf having 7–13 leaflets. Urushiol, the oil in the sap of these plants, is responsible for the rash. Within 14 hours of exposure, raised lines and/or blisters will appear on the affected area, accompanied by a terrible itch. Refrain from scratching, because bacteria under your fingernails can cause an infection. Wash and dry the affected area thoroughly, applying a calamine lotion to help dry out the rash. If itching or blistering is severe, seek medical attention. If you do come into contact with one of these plants, remember that oil-contami-nated clothes, hiking gear, and pets can easily cause an irritating rash on you or someone else, so wash not only any exposed parts of your body but also any exposed clothes, gear, and pets.

Mosquitoes

Ward off these pests with insect repellent or repellent-impregnated clothing. In some areas, mosquitoes are known to carry the West Nile virus, so all due caution should be taken to avoid their bites.

Snakes

Rattlesnakes, cottonmouths, copperheads, and corals are among the most common venomous snakes in the United States, and hiberna-tion season is typically October–April. Rattlesnakes like to bask in the sun and won't bite unless threatened.

In the region described in this book, you will possibly encoun-ter copperheads, rattlesnakes, and cottonmouths (sometimes referred to as water moccasins). However, the snakes you most likely will see while hiking will be nonvenomous species and subspecies. The best rule is to leave all snakes alone, give them a wide berth as you hike past, and make sure any hiking companions (including dogs) do the same.

When hiking, stick to well-used trails, and wear over-the-ankle boots and loose-fitting long pants. Do not step or put your hands beyond your range of detailed visibility, and avoid wandering around in the dark. Step *onto* logs and rocks, never *over* them, and be especially careful when climbing rocks. Always avoid walking through dense brush or willow thickets.

Black Bears

Though attacks by black bears are uncommon, the sight or approach of a bear can give anyone a start. If you encounter a bear while hiking, remain calm and avoid running in any direction. Make loud noises to scare off the bear and back away slowly. In primitive and remote areas, assume bears are present; in more developed sites, check on the current bear situation prior to hiking. Most encounters are food related, as bears have an exceptional sense of smell and not particularly discriminating tastes. While this is of greater concern to backpackers and campers, on a day hike, you may plan a lunchtime picnic or will munch on a power bar or other snack from time to time. So remain aware and alert.

Hunting

SEPARATE RULES, REGULATIONS, AND LICENSES govern the various hunting types and related seasons. Deer seasons typically coincide with prime hiking months in the fall and winter. Be sure to wear hunter orange and you shouldn't have a problem.

Regulations

PETS MUST BE LEASHED IN THE NATIONAL FORESTS and other jurisdictions included in this guide. In rare instances, pets are not permitted. These areas include specific parks and campgrounds along Arkansas's Buffalo National River. Check regulations for the area where you plan to hike. In Missouri, no pets are allowed on the Johnson's Shut-Ins Trail.

Hunting and fishing require the appropriate license for Arkansas and Missouri.

Some of the hikes in this guide are in wilderness areas. Wilderness areas do not have developed campgrounds. Mechanized vehicles and equipment are not permitted. Hunting, fishing, hiking, and open camping are all allowed. Map reading and orienteering skills are a necessity. More rules, maps, and information about wilderness areas can be found at wilderness.net.

Trail Etiquette

ALWAYS TREAT THE TRAIL, wildlife, and fellow hikers with respect. Here are some reminders.

★ Plan ahead in order to be self-sufficient at all times. For example, carry necessary supplies for changes in weather or other conditions. A well-planned trip brings satisfaction to you and to others.

★ Hike on open trails only. In seasons or construction areas where road or trail closures may be a possibility, use the websites, phone numbers, or e-mail addresses shown in the "Contacts" section at the beginning of each hike profile to check conditions prior to heading out for your hike. And don't attempt to circumvent such closures.

★ Don't trespass on private land, and obtain all permits and authorization as required. Leave gates as you found them or as directed by signage.

★ Be courteous to other hikers, bikers, equestrians, and others you encounter on the trails.

★ Never spook wild animals or pets. An unannounced approach, a sudden movement, or a loud noise startles most critters, and a surprised animal can be dangerous to you, to others, and to itself. Give animals plenty of space.

★ Observe the YIELD signs around the region's trailheads and backcountry. Typically, they advise hikers to yield to horses, and bikers yield to both horses and hikers. By common courtesy, on hills, hikers and bikers yield to any uphill traffic. When encountering mounted riders or horse packers, hikers can courteously step off the trail, on the downhill side if possible. So the horse can see and hear you, calmly greet the riders before they reach you and do not dart behind trees. Also resist the urge to pet horses unless you are invited to do so.

★ Stay on the existing trail and do not blaze any new trails.

★ Be sure to pack out what you pack in, leaving only your footprints. No one likes to see the trash someone else has left behind.

Tips on Enjoying Hiking in the Ozarks

PERMITS AND FEES ARE NOT REQUIRED IN THE OZARKS other than minimal day-use or parking fees. Trail and road conditions are the greatest concerns related to hiking in the Ozarks. The following contacts can be helpful as you plan to hike in the Ozarks of Arkansas and Missouri. The condition of isolated forest roads and trails can change quickly, as can creek levels, depending on precipitation. Acquiring current information can help you have a successful and fun trip.

Visit the Ozark Highlands Trail Association (OHTA) website for trail conditions related to the Ozarks of Arkansas: ozarkhighlandstrail.com. Under the contacts tab, you will find members listed who can provide current information about trail and road conditions in the areas you'll be hiking. Consider joining this organization that works to build and maintain the Ozark Trail, as well as many other area trails. A link to the OHTA Facebook page is also available from the website.

Go to the Arkansas Highway and Transportation Department website for information about road conditions: idrivearkansas.com.

Visit the Ozark–St. Francis National Forest website for supplemental information about the Ozarks and alerts related to the Ozark region: www.fs.usda.gov/osfnf.

Visit the Ozark Trail Association (OTA) website for trail conditions in the Ozarks of Missouri: ozarktrail.com. Consider joining this organization that builds and maintains the Ozark Trail. A link to the OTA Facebook page is on the website. Posing trail-related questions often generates some good responses from hikers with current knowledge of the trails.

Go to the Missouri Department of Transportation for current road conditions: traveler.modot.org/map. The map posted on the website provides valuable information in an easy-to-read format.

Visit the Mark Twain National Forest website for information and alerts related to the Ozarks of Missouri: www.fs.usda.gov/mtnf.

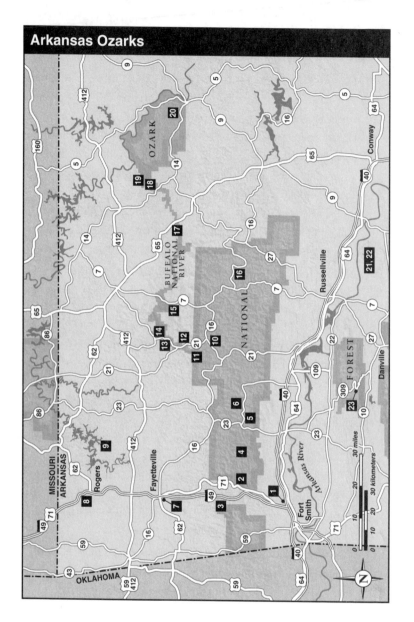

Arkansas Ozarks

Arkansas

Lake Alma Trail

SCENERY: ★ ★ ★ ★ ★
TRAIL CONDITION: ★ ★ ★
CHILDREN: ★ ★ ★ ★
DIFFICULTY: ★ ★ ★
SOLITUDE: ★ ★ ★

MCWATER FALLS IS A POPULAR STOP FOR LAKE ALMA TRAIL HIKERS.

GPS TRAILHEAD COORDINATES: N35° 29.818' W94° 13.073'

DISTANCE AND CONFIGURATION: 4.4-mile loop

HIKING TIME: 3 hours

HIGHLIGHTS: Waterfall, lake views, and historical rock structures

ELEVATION: 545' at trailhead, 594' at highest point

ACCESS: Open 24/7; no fees or permits required

MAPS: USGS *Alma* and *Mountainburg SW*

FACILITIES: Restrooms and picnic area (restrooms closed during winter)

WHEELCHAIR ACCESS: No

COMMENTS: The 1.6-mile out-and-back to McWater Falls is just right for children and novice hikers. Pets are allowed. This trail uses round yellow trail markers. The spur trail to the waterfall is marked with round orange markers.

CONTACTS: facebook.com/LakeAlmaTrail

Overview

Whether you're a parent looking for an easy day hike to introduce your children to the gentle pleasures of nature or a trail runner looking for a heart-throbbing good time, this loop hike is for you.

You'll see moss-covered boulder fields and historical rock structures up close. You'll walk beside clear streams, rocky cascades, and a 10-foot waterfall. Situated within a diverse mixed hardwood forest, you may spot deer, rabbit, fox, great blue heron, and a variety of songbirds and wildflowers.

Route Details

You'll be accessing the Lake Alma Trail by the paved walking path that connects to the parking area. As you begin walking, you'll see another paved path down below and closer to the lake on your left. You'll save that portion of pavement for the last part of your hike today. Note: There are mile markers on this trail, but they are approximate and based on distances calculated from the kiosk. The mileage is calculated beginning and ending at the parking area.

At mile 0.2, you'll arrive at the Lake Alma Trail kiosk. Where the pavement ends is where the work of volunteers begins. Volunteers built and installed this kiosk, and the trail logo was created by a young community volunteer.

The first section of the trail is easy walking. Follow the yellow trail markers. At mile 0.5, the trail turns to the right and goes up to cross a small drainage followed by easy walking until you arrive at the first bridge. The trail follows around the base of a hillside and then crosses a second bridge. If water is flowing under this bridge, the waterfall is something you'll want to see.

Take a right on the McWater Falls spur trail and follow orange trail markers, arriving at the waterfall at mile 0.8. If you backtrack and return to your car from here, this provides a nice 1.6-mile out-and-back hike for novice hikers. If you have young children,

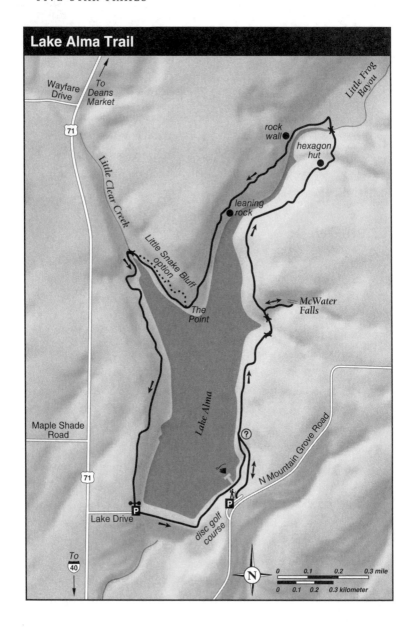

consider this option, and take your time returning to the trailhead. This waterfall was named for Harry McWater, the man who had the vision for this trail.

During the late 1990s, as a member of the Alma City Council, Harry brought up the possibility of a trail around the lake several times, only to be told that money for such a project wasn't available. In 2011, during a conversation with the mayor, he said, "What if I find volunteers to get that hiking trail built?" The mayor replied, "Go for it!" With that, Harry sought expertise and labor from the Arkansas Master Naturalists, the Ozark Highlands Trail Association, and local volunteers, including student organizations and scout troops. The trail began to see frequent use in the fall of 2012.

After enjoying McWater Falls, backtrack 0.1 mile to the main trail and turn right. You'll get glimpses of the lake in the distance on your left. At mile 1.0, you'll turn right onto an old roadbed. Watch to your right for some nice bluff areas and rock formations.

At 1.3 miles, you'll pass moss- and lichen-covered boulders that appear to have tumbled down the hillside on your right. Just past mile marker 1, you'll come to the hexagon hut. This homesite is a great place to explore, but please leave any historical artifacts in place. Mystery surrounds the construction of these structures and their occupants.

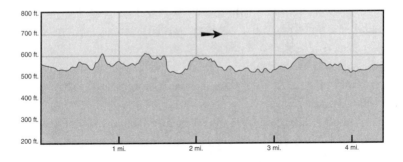

A DAY HIKER INSPECTS THE HEXAGON HOUSE NEXT TO THE TRAIL.

Pass the homesite on the old roadbed and turn left. If you walk into a gate, you missed the left turn. Watch for the round yellow markers. The trail goes down through a small rock wall and across a small drainage. The trail turns left and heads up a short, steep hill. You top out quickly and start down, turning left toward the bridge across Little Frog Bayou at 1.7 miles.

Take a left after the bridge, and then another left a few yards down the trail. Now you're walking down Little Frog Bayou toward the lake. A nice view of Little Frog Bayou opens up after you pass through an area thick with privet hedges. Following is a short climb to a rock wall on the right. Continue on this former road that looks and feels like a trail.

At 2.1 miles, you leave the roadbed and follow the trail down to the left. There is some rocky tread ahead in several spots, so watch your step. You'll pass a large leaning rock on the left and then descend to a tree with two yellow arrow markers, one pointing uphill to the right. Go left on the lower trail since the upper trail branches are not maintained and involve some scrambling. You may notice two more upper trail branches along this section, but in each case, you'll stay on the lower, maintained trail.

At 2.4 miles, you come to "The Point." There is a nice view back up to the dam and parking area where you began your hike. Here, an upper route climbs directly up and over a small bluffline (Little Snake Bluff) and then comes back down to the main trail. You'll follow the lower trail that stays close to the water. You're now walking up the Little Clear Creek that feeds Lake Alma on the northwest side. You'll come to a bridge at mile 2.7. Nice views appear up the creek and downstream to the east shoreline of the Lake Alma.

Take an immediate left at the end of the bridge and follow the creek downstream. You might see some numbered metal markers on trees in this area. In the 1980s, these markers indicated the locations of archery targets used in competition. The trail veers away from the water and crosses a drainage. At 2.9 miles, turn left onto an old roadbed. The footing is easy from here out, and the woods are nice.

At 3.3 miles, take another left onto a grassy, lightly used road. At 3.5 miles, you'll pass around a gate that brings you to a small parking area at the end of Lake Drive. This is an alternative access point to the trail from US 71. Cross the dam while taking in the view of the lake to the north, giving you an appreciation of the distance you've hiked.

Take a left at the end of the dam, heading north with the lake on your left. As you pass disc golf hole number 8, you may choose to veer right and return to the parking area. To do the whole trail, go straight down past a fishing pier. You're now on the lower paved path, heading toward the Lake Alma Trail kiosk. At the kiosk, take a right and return to the parking area at 4.4 miles.

Nearby Attractions

The Alma Aquatic Center has a swimming pool and waterslide. It's a great place for the kids to cool off after your hike (479-632-0700).

Fort Smith National Historic Site is operated by the National Park Service and provides tours of Judge Isaac Parker's Federal Courthouse and tells the stories of Federal Marshal Bass Reeves and other early lawmen. Wheelchair-accessible paths lead to the first fort site, River Park, and the out-and-back River Trail (479-783-3961).

Lake Fort Smith State Park has a beautiful campground with RV hookups, as well as cabins. It's also the beginning location for the Ozark Highlands Trail (479-369-2469; arkansasstateparks .com/lakefortsmith).

Directions

Take the Alma exit, Exit 13, off I-40, and drive north on US 71 to the first traffic light. Turn right onto Collum Lane East. Drive 0.2 mile and then left (north) on Mountain Grove Road. You might notice Lake Alma in the distance on your left as you drive on Collum Lane. Drive north on Mountain Grove Road 0.3 mile and take a left just past the two green water tanks. Drive down to the picnic area parking. The Lake Alma Trailhead is at the opening in the parking guardrail.

Lake Fort Smith
State Park: Shepherd Springs Loop

SCENERY: ★ ★ ★ ★ ★
TRAIL CONDITION: ★ ★ ★
CHILDREN: ★ ★ ★
DIFFICULTY: ★ ★ ★
SOLITUDE: ★ ★

SHEPHERD SPRINGS

GPS TRAILHEAD COORDINATES: N35° 41.735' W94° 07.108'

DISTANCE AND CONFIGURATION: 5.3-mile loop

HIKING TIME: 3 hours

HIGHLIGHTS: Lake views, waterfall, large rock formations, and historical homesites

ELEVATION: 973' at trailhead, 1,142' at highest point

ACCESS: 24/7; no fees or permits required

MAPS: USGS *Mountainburg*

FACILITIES: Restrooms and picnic area

WHEELCHAIR ACCESS: None

COMMENTS: A 3.6-mile out-and-back hike to historical Shepherd Springs is an option for younger children and novice hikers.

CONTACTS: Lake Fort Smith State Park, 479-369-2469, arkansasstateparks.com /lakefortsmith

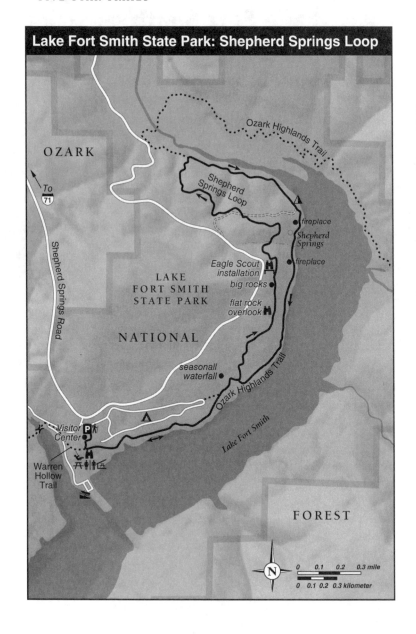

Lake Fort Smith State Park: Shepherd Springs Loop

OZARK

To 71

Ozark Highlands Trail

Shepherd Springs Loop

fireplace

Shepherd Springs

fireplace

LAKE FORT SMITH STATE PARK

Eagle Scout installation

big rocks

flat rock overlook

NATIONAL

Shepherd Springs Road

seasonall waterfall

Ozark Highlands Trail

Lake Fort Smith

Visitor Center

Warren Hollow Trail

FOREST

N

| 0 | 0.1 | 0.2 | 0.3 mile |
| 0 | 0.1 | 0.2 | 0.3 kilometer |

Overview

Here's a new loop trail the whole family will enjoy. This trail was completed in the spring of 2013 and follows a portion of the Ozark Highlands Trail (OHT), 200-plus miles long and growing. Don't worry though. You'll only be doing 5.3 miles on this loop route.

Begin with a tour through the Lake Fort Smith Visitor Center. Inside, you'll find 2,000 square feet of exhibits, including a bird-viewing area, a historical covered wagon, and a replica of the springs. Children may enjoy playing dress up with costumes representative of early settlers who occupied the area.

Route Details

This hike begins at the trailhead of the Ozark Highlands Trail located on the east side of the visitor center. The mileage is calculated from the rectangular OHT sign (nice photo op). Start walking down the winding sidewalk behind the visitor center. You'll pass Warren Hollow Trail on the right, one of several connecting trails in the park. Continue down the sidewalk, and you'll come to an overlook on the right. The large stones you're standing on as you look down on the lake are from the original Lake Fort Smith State Park, a few miles to the south. The new park was completed in May 2008 and included a new beginning route for the Ozark Highlands Trail.

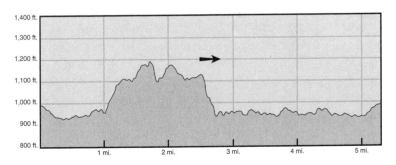

Shortly after the overlook, you'll leave the sidewalk and begin walking downhill and enter the woods. Watch for white blazes that mark the whole Ozark Highlands Trail. Portions of the campground will be visible uphill on your left. You'll pass through a series of small dips in the trail, some of which may contain water at different times of the year. At 0.9 mile, you'll arrive at a wet season waterfall. Immediately following is a drainage with large boulders. This is a great place to hang out for a break.

About 250 feet past the waterfall, you arrive at the SHEPHERD SPRINGS LOOP sign. Turn left and follow blue blazes. The trail shadows the drainage you just crossed and then veers to the right, taking you well above the Ozark Highlands Trail. At 1.2 miles, the trail starts a steep climb up steps to the next bench. There are nice rock formations all along this section, as well as some BIG rocks and nice views down to the lake on the east side when the trees have no leaves.

At 1.4 miles, you arrive at a flat rock overlook, a restful spot after the earlier climb. Look across Lake Fort Smith to the northeast and you'll see the inlet of Jack Creek in the distance. Continue along the bench trail with views of the lake to the southeast. The trail passes right next to a tall rock and then, about 50 yards later, comes into a rocky maze.

Blue blazes are nicely placed to keep you on the trail. Members of the Ozark Highlands Trail Association installed these blazes shortly after the trail was built. The 2-by-6-inch metal blazes were acquired from a company that manufactures window blinds.

At 1.6 miles, you come to an overlook and a wooden bench installed as part of an Eagle Scout project in July 2013. Step down from this level to a lower bench and several easy up and downs while trending downward. You'll be pleased not to be climbing in the opposite direction.

Continuing down to mile 1.8, you'll cross a little drainage and then climb slightly and level out. At 2.0 miles, you'll cross a roadbed, taking a left and then an immediate right, back onto the trail. There are a few ups and downs, typical Arkansas hiking. Eventually, you level off onto a bench. You'll hike down a steep incline with some steps placed intermittently. A few switchbacks might have been good in this area, but the trail builders chose a more direct route, so watch your step. At 2.2 miles, you'll cross and then walk along the side of a deep valley for a short time. The trail moves away from the valley and then goes through some nice, open woods before descending to the Ozark Highlands Trail.

At just past 2.6 miles, you arrive at the Ozark Highlands Trail. Turn right (east). You're now following white trail blazes again and heading back toward the trailhead. To the left are views down to the lake. There are few blazes on this old road that used to lead to Lake Shepherd Springs, now part of a larger Lake Fort Smith. You'll stay on the roadbed for a while. At 3.3 miles, you come to a campsite and turn right, leaving this roadbed and moving into the woods. The trail immediately swings back to the left, continuing along the lake.

An old fireplace is beside the trail at 3.4 miles. Hike about 250 feet farther and you'll arrive at the historical Shepherd Springs. You'll almost always find water in this spring, but filter before drinking. The Shepherd family arrived in this valley in 1840 and made improvements to this spring that have stood the test of time. The spring eventually took their name and became known as Shepherd Springs. There are lots of big boulders just past the spring, so watch your footing.

At 3.6 miles, you'll come to a second fireplace in the trail. Shortly past the fireplace, you'll come to an area covered with English ivy. The remains of a stone wall are just below the trail. Pause and think about the early occupants of this area. The lake would not have been here, but Frog Bayou could have been seen down in the valley. Imagine fetching your drinking water from Shepherd Springs.

You'll pass the intersection to the Shepherd Springs Trail you used earlier at 4.3 miles. Go straight and immediately past the waterfall. Continue on the trail hiked earlier back to the visitor center. You'll arrive at the trailhead and complete this 5.3-mile hike. Stop in at the visitor center and give the attendant an update on trail conditions.

You might enjoy the exhibits anew with your firsthand knowledge of the historical Shepherd Springs and surrounding area.

Nearby Attractions

Several other trails in Lake Fort Smith State Park lead to picnic and camping areas, cabins, and lodges. This park's master plan allows visitors to access all areas of the park on foot. These connecting trails are a pleasure to walk, so you might want to rent a cabin or campsite and stay awhile.

Boston Mountain Guest Ranch is located on US 71, 2.5 miles south of Shepherd Springs Road (479-369-2014).

Artist Point is 1 mile north of the intersection of Shepherd Springs Road and US 71 (479-369-2226). This historical gift shop houses a small American Indian museum and carries snacks and souvenirs.

Directions

The park is 20 miles north of Alma, and 32 miles south of Fayetteville. From I-49, take Exit 29 at Mountainburg and go east on AR 282 1.8 mile to US 71, and then drive north on US 71 7.5 miles to Shepherd Springs Road. Turn east on Shepherd Springs Road and go 2 miles to the park.

Devil's Den State Park:
Yellow Rock Trail

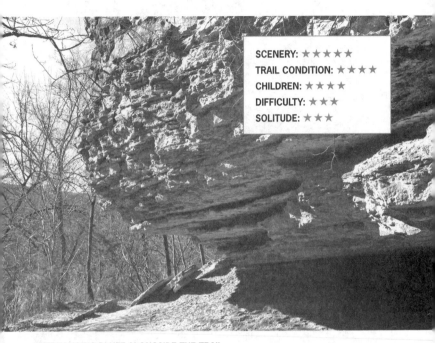

SCENERY: ★ ★ ★ ★ ★
TRAIL CONDITION: ★ ★ ★ ★
CHILDREN: ★ ★ ★ ★
DIFFICULTY: ★ ★ ★
SOLITUDE: ★ ★ ★

OVERHANGING BLUFF ALONGSIDE THE TRAIL

GPS TRAILHEAD COORDINATES: N35° 46.930' W94° 14.826'

DISTANCE AND CONFIGURATION: 3.2-mile balloon

HIKING TIME: 2.5 hours

HIGHLIGHTS: Grand vistas from Yellow Rock Bluff and Overlook Shelter

ELEVATION: 1,042' at trailhead, 1,420' at high point

ACCESS: 24/7; no fees or permits required

MAPS: USGS *Winslow* and *Strickler;* available in visitor center

FACILITIES: Restrooms, cabins, campground, restaurant open seasonally

WHEELCHAIR ACCESS: No

COMMENTS: Leashed pets are allowed.

CONTACTS: Devil's Den State Park, 479-761-3325, arkansasstateparks.com/devilsden

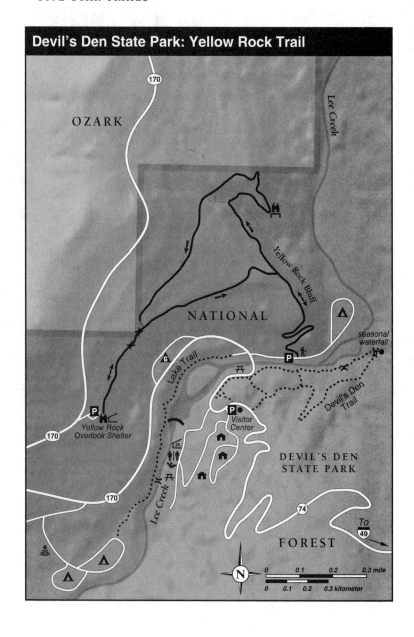

Devil's Den State Park: Yellow Rock Trail

Overview

This popular trail takes you to a beautiful bluff (Yellow Rock) over-looking the Lee Creek drainage. The trail will also take you to an overlook built in 1934 by the Civilian Conservation Corps (CCC). The views and the stone structures are highlights, as well as the small caves and crevices along the trail.

Route Details

The Yellow Rock Trail is marked with white triangles. The trail makes a few switchbacks up immediately and goes between two large bluffs with lots of unusual fissures and formations. At 0.2 mile, the trail skirts alongside and almost under a bluff with a small cave at its base. The trail then makes several tight switchbacks and begins following along a ledge revealing a view down to the right (southeast) from whence you came. To the left are open hardwoods with a few cedars mixed in.

You'll be hiking the loop section of this trail counterclockwise, so veer to the right at the intersection at 0.5 mile. During winter when the trees have no leaves, you'll be able to see Yellow Rock Bluff from here.

At 0.9 mile, the trail comes out onto Yellow Rock Bluff, tower-ing more than 300 feet over the Lee Creek drainage with expansive

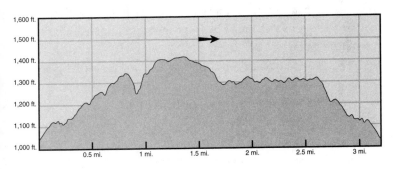

SMALL OUTCROP NEXT TO YELLOW ROCK BLUFF WITH VIEWS ACROSS LEE CREEK

views across the valley. This is a great scene to take in during every season. You'll never see it the same way twice.

Hike across the bluff to the north and back into the woods on the trail. You'll pass a small spur to a lesser bluff, a nice spot for lunch or a break. One more chance to take in the view!

At 1.0 mile, turn to the right (northeast). A lesser trail goes straight, but that is a shortcut you don't want to take. The trail to the right goes a short distance before taking a hard left to the southwest. The trail takes you past a small bluff and then up and over it. This is a great little spot not to be missed.

You'll be on top of a bench and walking level trail at 1.1 miles. After another 0.1 mile, you'll cross two little drains then return to level tread and a richer forested area with few cedars.

At 1.7 miles, take steps down to an intersection with a trail. Turn right (southwest), and follow this spur 0.3 mile to the overlook shelter. You'll cross two bridges as you move toward the overlook. Watch down to the left for the Lee Creek drainage and small lake, built by the CCC.

At 2.0 miles, you'll come to the Yellow Rock Overlook Shelter, a beautiful structure built by the CCC in 1934. A plaque states that CCC directors were so impressed with this shelter that they nominated it for a Pulitzer Award for Structures, but this was done in humor, as no such award existed.

After spending some time at the shelter taking in the views or having a picnic lunch, turn around and backtrack down the spur. At 2.2 miles, go straight past the intersection with the trail traveled earlier. Follow along the bench, hiking through a small cedar grove at 2.5 miles, where the trail veers right and descends, arriving at the intersection where you began your loop hike earlier. At 2.7 miles, go straight and backtrack the first section of trail, arriving at the trailhead and completing the hike at 3.2 miles.

Nearby Attractions

Lake Fort Smith State Park has a beautiful campground with RV hookups, as well as cabins. It's also the beginning location for the Ozark Highlands Trail (479-369-2469; arkansasstateparks.com /lakefortsmith).

Directions

If approaching from the south on I-49, after you pass through the Bobby Hopper Tunnel, take Exit 45 for Winslow and turn left (west) on AR 74. From the turnoff, it's 6.8 miles to the Devil's Den Visitor Center. At 4.5 miles, you'll pass the DEVIL'S DEN STATE PARK sign on the right. Continue down the steep switchbacks until you reach 6.8 miles and watch for the visitor center on the left. Stay to the right after the visitor center. You'll see the CAMPGROUND-A sign; turn right just past the Lee Creek bridge. Look for the Yellow Rock Trailhead on the left. Parking is on the opposite side of the road.

If driving from the north, from I-49, take AR 170 at West Fork, Exit 53, and drive 17 miles to the park. This is the best route if you're pulling a camper trailer.

White Rock Mountain:
Rim Trail

SCENERY: ★ ★ ★ ★ ★
TRAIL CONDITION: ★ ★ ★
CHILDREN: ★ ★ ★
DIFFICULTY: ★ ★
SOLITUDE: ★ ★ ★

THE BLUFFS OF WHITE ROCK MOUNTAIN NORTH OF SUNSET SHELTER

GPS TRAILHEAD COORDINATES: N35° 41.373' W93° 57.264'

DISTANCE AND CONFIGURATION: 2.1-mile loop

HIKING TIME: 1.5 hours

HIGHLIGHTS: Stunning views in all directions, sheer blufflines, and beautifully crafted stone shelters

ELEVATION: 2,319' at trailhead, 2,319' at highest point, 2,221' at lowest point

ACCESS: Open 24/7; no fees or permits required

MAPS: USGS *Bidville*

FACILITIES: Pit toilets in the campground. Be sure to bring water, especially if hiking in the winter when water might be turned off in the campground.

WHEELCHAIR ACCESS: No

COMMENTS: Leashed pets are allowed. Be cautious next to high bluffs.

CONTACTS: White Rock Mountain Cabins & Camping, 479-369-4128, whiterockmountain.com

Overview

You'll drive over 20 hilly miles, much of it gravel, to reach White Rock Mountain, but you'll be rewarded for your efforts as you reach this beautiful mountaintop. Allow plenty of time to walk this short loop trail because you'll find yourself gawking at views every step of the way. If you do this hike, glance at the trail often to ensure you don't stumble while being entranced by the views. There have been deaths as a result of falls from these bluffs.

You might want to spend a few days camping on White Rock Mountain and exploring this loop with your camera in a different light and at different times of the day. If you plan to stay in the rustic cabins, make reservations far in advance.

Route Details

Begin at the kiosk located at the end of the road past the cabins. These cabins are usually booked, and it's easy to see why with their views from the mountainside. Check the kiosk for any trail updates, and then begin walking down the trail. Pretty quickly you'll come to an intersection with the Shores Lake Loop to the right, but you'll go straight and stay on the Rim Trail.

Views open up down to the east into Bear Creek Hollow, Salt Creek drainage, and Potato Knob Mountain farther to the northeast. You'll enjoy stunning vistas throughout this hike on clear days. Watch your footing because the bluffs are high with uneven edges on top.

At 0.8 mile, you'll pass the first of four shelters built around the edges of White Rock Mountain. Stop and enjoy the views. At 1.0 mile, you cross Bowles Gap Road and continue on the trail a few feet to the left on the other side of the road, now walking on the west side of the mountain.

Pretty soon you'll come to the West Shelter at about 1.2 miles. Each of these shelters is a treat to see, and the views are amazing.

The Sunset Shelter at 1.7 miles is a great spot to see the sunrise and sunset. Markers on the rock wall to the west of the shelter point toward area towns in the distance to give you a perspective of the distances you're viewing. Soon you'll pass the South Shelter with views to the south down the White Rock Creek drainage and Shores Lake area. The rustic cabins, built in the 1930s, are up above the trail at this point.

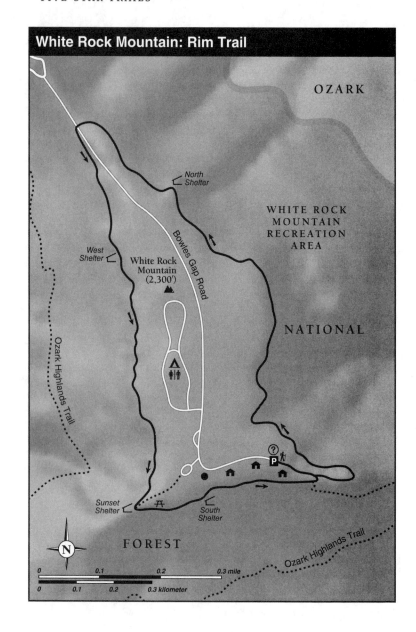

White Rock Mountain: Rim Trail

OZARK

North
Shelter

WHITE ROCK
MOUNTAIN
RECREATION
AREA

West
Shelter

White Rock
Mountain
(2,300')

Bowles Gap Road

Ozark Highlands Trail

NATIONAL

Sunset
Shelter

South
Shelter

FOREST

Ozark Highlands Trail

N

| 0 | 0.1 | 0.2 | 0.3 mile |

| 0 | 0.1 | 0.2 | 0.3 kilometer |

Continue down the trail to mile 2.0, and you'll reach the intersection with the short spur where you began your hike. Turn left and hike back up to the trailhead to complete this 2.1-mile hike.

Nearby Attractions

White Rock Mountain Cabins and Campground provides tent camping, as well as cabins. Walking out the back door of any of the rustic cabins puts you on the White Rock Mountain Loop (479-369-4128; whiterockmountain.com).

Directions

Take Exit 24 from I-40 and drive north on AR 215 9.0 miles to Fern. Follow AR 215 right at 9.4 miles. At 12.2 miles, drive straight, leaving AR 215 and continuing on Bliss Ridge Road. Continue past Shores Lake Campground on Bliss Ridge Road (dirt) for 4.0 miles, then turn left onto White Rock Mountain Road. After 2.2 miles on White Rock Mountain Road, turn right and drive the final 1.0 mile up to White Rock Mountain. Continue driving past the White Rock Mountain Campground, the caretaker's residence, and cabins. The White Rock Mountain Loop Trailhead is at the end of the road. The total driving distance from I-40 is approximately 21 miles.

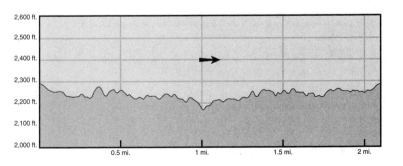

Redding Loop and Spy Rock Trail

SCENERY: ★ ★ ★ ★ ★
TRAIL CONDITION: ★ ★ ★ ★ ★
CHILDREN: ★ ★
DIFFICULTY: ★ ★ ★
SOLITUDE: ★ ★ ★

REDDING LOOP WATERFALL FLOWING STRONGLY DURING WET SEASON

GPS TRAILHEAD COORDINATES: N35° 40.925' W93° 47.154'

DISTANCE AND CONFIGURATION: 8.3-mile loop

HIKING TIME: 5 hours

HIGHLIGHTS: Spy Rock view and two wet-season waterfalls and views down into the Mulberry Valley

ELEVATION: 856' at trailhead, 1,833' at high point

ACCESS: 24/7; $3 per vehicle for day use at trailhead

MAPS: USGS *Cass*

FACILITIES: Restrooms and campground

WHEELCHAIR ACCESS: No

COMMENTS: You could access Spy Rock as a 7.8-mile out-and-back using the east route, but the distance is close to the loop mileage. It's recommended to do the whole loop and see it all.

CONTACTS: Ozark National Forest, Pleasant Hill Ranger District, 479-754-2864, tinyurl.com/reddingloop

Overview

This trail provides access to a beautiful, expansive view on a well-built trail. You'll hike past two wet-season waterfalls and nice views into the Mulberry Valley.

Route Details

Begin this hike at Redding Campground behind campsite 20, across the road from the restrooms. Follow blue blazes east into a flat, open section of pine forest. At 0.5 mile, you'll come to an intersection and trail register box. Take a left (north), and head up the east loop, following a small seasonal creek on your right. After crossing AR 215, you'll hike up into a pine cedar mix with a small creek on the right side. You'll eventually veer away from the creek.

The trail follows a ridge with nice views in fall and winter. You'll see Spy Rock bluff to the northeast. In another hour or so, you'll be taking in the views from that bluff. At 1.7 miles, you'll have a clear view of Spy Rock on your left. The first of several wildlife food plots is up above the trail. The trail drops off this ridge and follows along the hillside for a while. At 2.8 miles, the trail crosses County Road 82.

At 3.0 miles, take a left on a spur trail. Views down to the right are of Herrods Creek drainage. The intersection of the Spy Rock spur trail is at 3.5 miles. Take a left (southwest) and follow this trail, arriving at Spy Rock overlook at 3.9 miles. Stay well away from the edge, as a fall would probably be fatal. Legend has it that Spanish explorers hid gold nearby and used this bluff to be sure no one was watching. No gold has ever been found, but if you're visiting in the fall, you'll see some vibrant gold foliage down below and across the mountains in the distance.

If you pack in water, this is a nice campsite for stargazing. After taking in the views or lunch, backtrack to Redding Loop. The hiking always seems faster when you're backtracking, and you'll enjoy some of the great views down into Herrods Creek valley twice. Be sure to turn right at the intersection with the spur trail, so you don't end up

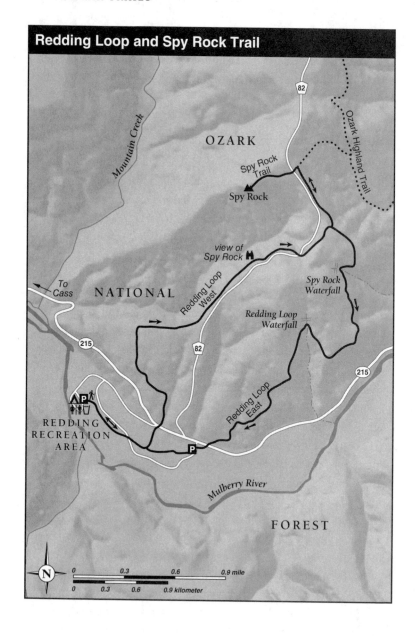

Redding Loop and Spy Rock Trail

OZARK

Mountain Creek

82

Ozark Highland Trail

Spy Rock Trail

Spy Rock

view of Spy Rock

Spy Rock Waterfall

To Cass

NATIONAL

Redding Loop West

Redding Loop Waterfall

82

215

215

Redding Loop East

REDDING RECREATION AREA

P

Mulberry River

FOREST

N

| 0 | 0.3 | 0.6 | 0.9 mile |
| 0 | 0.3 | 0.6 | 0.9 kilometer |

hiking another 100 or so miles on the Ozark Highlands Trail by accident. At 4.7 miles, you'll take a left back onto Redding Loop.

To the northeast, at mile 5.0, the view opens up to the Mulberry Valley on your left. You'll cross a deep drain with a wet-season waterfall on a moss-covered bluff. This is a beautiful area to explore. More views into the Mulberry Valley follow, along with a pine grove and another wildlife food plot up above the trail. This section has a lot of level walking.

At 6.0 miles, you approach a deep drain with an 8-foot waterfall. The trail crosses over the top of the waterfall. When water is flowing, this waterfall will be worth the trip by itself. Continue to walk the ridge with the valley on your left past yet another food plot.

At 6.5 miles, the trail begins a winding descent toward AR 215. You'll pass through another pine grove and across a small glade area, eventually crossing the highway and continuing into the woods on the other side. Take a left on the small gravel road you come to shortly after AR 215. This brings you to a second trailhead and kiosk for Redding Loop. This parking area is free and a good option if you're not using Redding Campground, which has camping and day-use fees.

Walk through the parking area of the alternate trailhead and follow the blue blazes back into the woods. At 7.7 miles, the trail

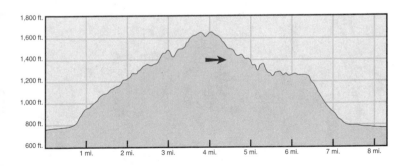

comes to the east–west sign and the trail register box. Now you're backtracking the final 0.5 mile to Redding Campground to complete your 8.3-mile hike.

Nearby Attractions

Turner Bend Store carries groceries and supplies and serves up great sandwiches. It also has camping facilities and boat rentals (479-667-3641; turnerbend.com).

The Oark General Store first opened in 1890 and is listed on the Arkansas Register of Historic Places. You'll find great posthike food and a few grocery items (479-292-3351; oarkgeneralstore.com).

Directions

From the town of Ozark on I-40, take Exit 35. Drive north on AR 23 11.5 miles past Turner Bend Store, and then another 1.5 miles to the little town of Cass. Just past Cass, turn right onto AR 215 East. Drive 2.7 miles east and turn right at the Redding Campground entrance. The trail begins behind campsite 20 across the road from the campground showers and restrooms.

Marinoni Scenic Area

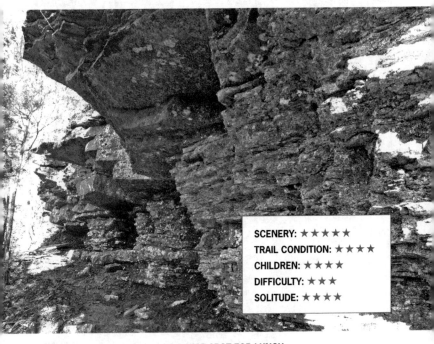

SCENERY: ★ ★ ★ ★ ★
TRAIL CONDITION: ★ ★ ★ ★
CHILDREN: ★ ★ ★ ★
DIFFICULTY: ★ ★ ★
SOLITUDE: ★ ★ ★ ★

THIS TRAILSIDE BLUFF PROVIDES A NICE SPOT FOR LUNCH.

GPS TRAILHEAD COORDINATES: N35° 41.043' W93° 42.612'

DISTANCE AND CONFIGURATION: 5.4-mile out-and-back

HIKING TIME: 4 hours

HIGHLIGHTS: Tall bluffs, Briar Branch, waterfalls, scenic valleys, and rock ledges with spectacular views

ELEVATION: 816' at trailhead, 1,405' at highest point

ACCESS: Open 24/7; no fees or permits required

MAPS: USGS *Yale*

FACILITIES: None

WHEELCHAIR ACCESS: No

COMMENTS: The Dawna Robinson Indian Creek Spur Trail allows access to one of the most beautiful places in Arkansas.

CONTACTS: Turner Bend Store, 479-667-3641, turnerbend.com/store; Ozark Highlands Trail Association, ozarkhighlandstrail.com

Marinoni Scenic Area

Overview

Imagine a place with twisting waterfalls, arching rock bluffs, and towering trees. Walk along a gentle stream that flows over rocks into quiet, clear pools. Leave your cell phone in the car because there's no coverage here, and who wants to hear digital sounds in this acoustic setting? You'll want to have your camera batteries fully charged. This out-and-back day hike offers numerous photo ops as you walk along beautiful Briar Branch.

Route Details

You'll access the Marinoni Scenic Area by way of the Dawna Robinson Indian Creek Spur Trail. The spur trail is marked with 2-by-6-inch blue metal blazes. From the Indian Creek Canoe Launch parking area, look across AR 215 to an opening in the fence with a blue blaze and a small trail sign. Don't let the appearance of the entrance dissuade you from walking this trail. What you'll find beyond this opening in a barbed wire fence is some of Arkansas's richest beauty.

As you step past the fence opening, take a left and follow the trail, watching on the right for a stone marker placed in memory of Dawna Robinson. She was a trail maintainer and volunteer, of whom Mike Lemaster, former president of the Ozark Highlands Trail

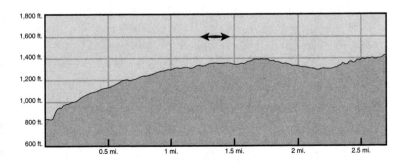

Association (OHTA), said, "Dawna's spirited personality and dedication came to mind as a fitting tribute to memorialize the hard work and perseverance of volunteers."

Just past the marker, you'll begin a short climb up several switchbacks, passing the base of a small overhanging bluff. The trail you're walking on was built by OHTA volunteers in March 2011. This little bluff area was a favorite lunch spot during that week of hard work. Enjoy the view down into the Indian Creek valley.

The switchbacks top out into open woods and easy walking. You might catch a glimpse of the parking area and Mulberry River down to your right. At 0.6 mile, turn left onto an old roadbed that appears to get some four-wheeler use. Then turn to the right (east) onto the Ozark Highlands Trail (OHT). The blazes are now white. You'll pass OHT mile marker 52 almost immediately.

You're hiking with Briar Branch down on the right with views of mountains and bluffs across to the southeast. You'll pass a number of small drainages, but they're dry most of the year. For the next couple of miles, follow this ridge with easy walking in a mixed pine-hardwood forest.

There are a couple of little rock ledges at 1.5 miles overlooking the Briar Branch drainage. They're great places for a little quiet time or snack—you might need one of these spots on your return trip out.

At mile marker 53 of the OHT, you'll see a small rock outcrop just left of the trail. In wet winter conditions, this rock displays interesting ice formations. A few yards later, you'll cross a faint roadbed that once took a very direct route down to the creek. I would hesitate to drive a jeep down this steep incline, much less a vehicle from earlier times.

At 2.0 miles, Briar Branch comes into view down on the southeast side of the trail. You'll be following this creek for a while. As you come down to creek level, you'll pass two campsites. These are nice places for a break with easy access to water. This out-and-back hike is a wonderful backpacking trip for families with children if you're looking for overnight options in the future. Be sure to take good care of this fragile area.

INDIAN CREEK VALLEY AS SEEN FROM THE DAWNA ROBINSON INDIAN CREEK SPUR TRAIL

Continuing up Briar Branch, you'll cross at 2.3 miles and begin walking with the creek down to your left. Time to get the camera out if it isn't already. The trail will climb a little along a ridge with large bluffs to your right. Pay attention to your footing because it's a steep slide down if you fall from the trail while gawking at the sights. At 2.4 miles, walk over the top of a twisting waterfall. A small spur takes you down to the base of the falls.

The Marinoni historic marker is just past OHT mile marker 54 at mile 2.7 of the hike. Paul A. Marinoni was from Fayetteville and a friend of Tim Ernst's father. Tim, renowned outdoor photographer and author of the *Ozark Highlands Trail Guide,* said, "My dad had his first heart attack when I was only 6, so he was unable to take me to the woods like he would have wanted to. When I was 7, I began spending a lot of time with Paul Marinoni, hunting and camping during annual retreats into the woods. Paul was a real character, one of the most down-to-earth and honest people you would ever meet." Given Tim's sentiments, it seemed proper to name this area after a man who influenced others to appreciate the Ozarks.

A small cave, located just past the Marinoni marker, is a great place for children to explore. A cascade flows down the hillside and crosses the trail here, making a pleasant lunch spot before beginning the hike back to the trailhead by the same way you came. If you have the urge to explore, a natural bridge is a short distance farther down the trail at the top of the bluff.

Backtrack to the trailhead to complete this 5.4-mile hike. As you descend toward the trailhead on your last 0.5 mile, be sure to pause at the little bluff in the switchbacks and reflect on the beauty of the Marinoni Scenic Area. You won't want this hike to end.

Nearby Attractions

Turner Bend Store carries groceries and supplies and serves up great sandwiches. It also has camping facilities and boat rentals (479-667-3641; turnerbend.com).

The Oark General Store first opened in 1890 and is listed on the Arkansas Register of Historic Places. You'll find great posthike food and a few grocery items (479-292-3351; oarkgeneralstore.com).

Directions

From the town of Ozark on I-40, take Exit 35. Drive north on AR 23 11.5 miles past Turner Bend Store, and then another 1.5 miles to the little town of Cass. Just past Cass, turn right onto AR 215 East. Travel 7.4 miles to the Indian Creek Canoe Launch and OHT Access. The trail is on the north side of the highway and begins at an opening in the fence directly across from the INDIAN CREEK OHT ACCESS sign.

7

Kessler Mountain Trails

SCENERY: ★ ★ ★ ★ ★
TRAIL CONDITION: ★ ★ ★ ★
CHILDREN: ★ ★ ★
DIFFICULTY: ★ ★ ★ ★
SOLITUDE: ★ ★ ★

THE ROCK CITY SLOTS ARE GREAT FUN FOR HIKERS AND MOUNTAIN BIKERS.

GPS TRAILHEAD COORDINATES: N36° 01.648' W94° 11.869'

DISTANCE AND CONFIGURATION: 10-mile balloon with multiple loops and out-and-back spur

HIKING TIME: 6 hours

HIGHLIGHTS: Massive rock maze, house-size boulders, and expansive views

ELEVATION: 1,298' at trailhead, 1,894' at highest point

ACCESS: Open 24/7; no fees or permits required

MAPS: USGS *Fayetteville*

FACILITIES: Restrooms and Kessler Mountain Regional Park athletic fields near the trailhead

WHEELCHAIR ACCESS: No

COMMENTS: Leashed pets are allowed. You'll have cell phone coverage throughout this hike. This trail is open to mountain bikes, so stay alert and listen for approaching bicycles. An alternate trailhead that gives access to Rock City is located on US 62 at the Fayettechill Outlet.

CONTACTS: Mount Kessler Greenways, 479-957-4069, mtkesslergreenways.com; Kessler Mountain Regional Park, fayetteville-ar.gov/1976/Kessler-Mountain-Regional-Park

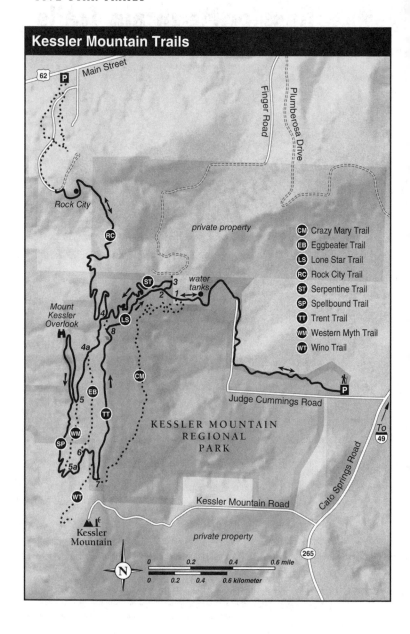

Kessler Mountain Trails

CM	Crazy Mary Trail
EB	Eggbeater Trail
LS	Lone Star Trail
RC	Rock City Trail
ST	Serpentine Trail
SP	Spellbound Trail
TT	Trent Trail
WM	Western Myth Trail
WT	Wino Trail

KESSLER MOUNTAIN
REGIONAL
PARK

Overview

This system of trails is largely due to the efforts of Frank Sharp, who built a coalition around protecting Kessler Mountain as a green space on the edge of the thriving city of Fayetteville. The combination of trails described here will lead you on paths named Rock City and Spellbound. These names accurately describe the beauty you'll find.

Hiking Kessler Mountain gives you the ability to come off the trail and select from a wide variety of local restaurants for a posthike meal. Fayetteville is also a great place to stay awhile, with lodging, shopping, and entertainment options available.

Route Details

The trail begins at the parking area. There are no blazes on any of these trails, but intersections are marked with signs. Intersection numbers are only for reference to the map on the facing page; intersections are not numbered on the trail. Kessler Mountain Regional Park construction will continue and trail developments are ongoing. Improvements should be clearly marked and easy to follow.

The first part of the trail is fairly level, skirting private property at the beginning. You'll pass through some briar patches, but they are usually cut well away from the trail. You'll also pass through some small cedar patches early in the trail.

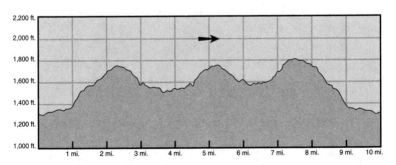

At 1.0 mile, you'll find yourself in an oak hardwood forest that is fairly open and level. If not for the highway sound from the east, you'd think you were in deep woods, but you're close to civilization.

A small roadbed intersects the trail, but continue straight across on the trail. That abandoned road goes a short distance to a small pond on private property. At 1.1 miles, you'll come to a gravel road and turn north (right) onto the road. Walking this uphill road isn't bad because of the nice woods on both sides. You'll see some rock walls out in the woods.

At 1.4 miles, you'll come to a fenced area containing two large water tanks. Turn left (southwest) off the gravel road and walk along the fence, then right (northwest) and quickly reenter the woods. Follow the signs.

At 1.5 miles, reach the first trail intersection (1). Stay straight and slightly to your right. The sign says CRAZY MARY and PARK OVERLOOK, but you're going to Rock City using the Serpentine Trail. Walk a short distance to the second trail intersection (2). The sign says CRAZY MARY and you'll turn right. Later, you'll come down from the mountain on the Lone Star Trail, which is on the left at this junction, but there might not be a sign for it. Turn right on Crazy Mary, and come almost immediately to intersection 3 at 1.7 miles. Turn left (northwest) to follow the Serpentine Trail. Avoid the lesser trail that continues straight. The Serpentine Trail is a tight, winding path that works itself gradually up the mountain, passing through large beech trees, white oak, and a variety of hardwoods.

You're in some beautiful open woods at 1.8 miles. These switchbacks are nice and tight and bicycle friendly, but they also make this climb up the mountainside a pleasure. This section is very kid friendly since you're not climbing at a steep pitch.

At mile 2.4, take a right (northwest) and walk 25 yards to the Rock City intersection (intersection 4). The sign says ROCK CITY, SPELLBOUND, EGGBEATER, WESTERN MYTH. To this point, you've been hiking on the east side of the mountain. At intersection 4, take a right (north) to Rock City. You'll be on this trail for a while going out and back. You're now walking along a ridge with the mountain dropping away on both sides. The trail is rocky in spots, so you'll want to watch your footing.

Shortly the trail turns right off the ridge and then switchbacks around over to the west side of the mountain and begins to switchback downward. At 2.9 miles, you'll come alongside a barbed wire fence and pass under a power line. At 3.4 miles, you come to the edge of a ridge with views down into the valley, and you'll see more rocky bluffs up on your right.

You'll soon pass through two small boulder stacks that seem to be acting as gates to Rock City because you begin to see more interesting rock formations with every step after passing between them. There are many large broken boulder formations to see, and it's time to get the camera out. You'll see several overlooks with suitable sitting spots for a break.

You'll come to a left turn and follow down some rocky footing to the next bench at 3.7 miles. Then you'll enter Rock City proper, a rocky maze with towering boulders all around. You'll come to a fence with a gravel road on the other side at 3.9 miles. Here is where you begin to backtrack. The trail turns sharply left and begins downhill, but you're going to turn around here and pass back through the rocky maze and then head toward the Spellbound Trail. It's a pleasure to hike Rock City Trail out and back because it's a visual treat every step of the way.

At 5.3 miles, you'll arrive back at intersection 4 where you began the out-and-back to Rock City. Now you'll turn right toward Spellbound and Western Myth Trails. At 5.5 miles, you'll come to intersection 4a for Western Myth and Spellbound. Take a right (veering south) and leave Eggbeater Trail, which continues straight ahead.

After following Western Myth a short distance, you'll come to intersection 5 with Spellbound at 5.8 miles. Turn right (southwest) onto Spellbound. Staying straight is Western Myth. Follow Spellbound to the north, with views down into Fayetteville on your left. At 6.1 miles, you'll arrive at a nice flat rock overlook, but there are

SIGNS MARK THE MANY TRAIL INTERSECTIONS ON KESSLER MOUNTAIN.

many nice views all along the trail and many "take a break" rocks. Spellbound is what you'll be as you take in the views and boulders all around.

At 6.7 miles, the trail begins to switchback to a higher level, coming to an intersection (intersection 5a, Spellbound–Western Myth) at just past 6.8 miles. Climb 0.2 mile to the next intersection with Eggbeater, arriving at intersection 6 for Eggbeater and Spellbound at 7.0 miles. Continue straight (northwest) on Spellbound. Do not take a left onto Eggbeater.

You'll come to a pretty good climb and pass the Wino spur on the right, but continue straight. Just past that intersection there is a nice stone bench.

At intersection 7, you'll come to the Crazy Mary and Trent Trails. Here there is also a trail that comes in from the right. Turn left (north) onto Trent Trail at mile 7.2. This is ridgetop walking and pretty level. You'll make good time on this wide-topped mountain. You'll hear interstate traffic off to the east and see some glimpses of valleys on both sides in fall and winter, but no expansive views. The Trent Trail is a nice, relaxing walk in the woods.

At 7.9 miles, a TRENT TRAIL sign indicates to veer right, leaving an old roadbed that turns slightly to the left. The trail comes alongside a little pond, the only water on this route during dry seasons. The murky water is welcomed by trail dogs but wouldn't be suitable for drinking without some serious filtering.

At 8.0 miles, you'll come to intersection 8, with a sign directing you to the water tanks via Lone Star Trail. After some downhill, you'll come to an intersection at 8.3 miles that says CRAZY MARY. Take a right (southeast) and begin backtracking downhill on the original trail you hiked at the beginning of your climb up the mountain.

At 8.4 miles, you'll pass a junction for park overlooks, water tanks, and Crazy Mary. Stay straight, heading down toward the water tanks. At 8.5 miles, just past the two water tanks, take a right onto Judge Cummings Road that you traveled earlier.

Continue backtracking, watching for the sign directing you left and back into the woods from the gravel road at 8.8 miles. You'll arrive back at the trailhead and parking area to complete this 10-mile hike.

Nearby Attractions

The City of Fayetteville has restaurants and shopping, as well as a lively nightlife scene on Dixon Street, a few blocks from the University of Arkansas (479-521-1316; fayetteville-ar.gov).

Northwest Arkansas Trails Razorback Greenways has developed a series of trails connecting the city of Fayetteville with Springdale, Bentonville, and Rogers. These are open to foot traffic but ideal for biking. Maps are available at nwatrails.org.

Directions

From I-49 in Fayetteville, take Exit 60 and turn south onto AR 265 (Cato Springs Road). Drive 0.6 mile and turn right onto Judge Cummings Road (County Road 200). Drive 0.2 mile to the Kessler Mountain parking area and trailhead.

8

Crystal Bridges Museum of American Art Loop

SCENERY: ★ ★ ★ ★
TRAIL CONDITION: ★ ★ ★ ★ ★
CHILDREN: ★ ★ ★ ★ ★
DIFFICULTY: ★ ★
SOLITUDE: ★ ★

VISITORS ENJOY THE SHADE OF THE TULIP TREE SHELTER.

GPS TRAILHEAD COORDINATES: N36° 22.899' W94° 12.156'

DISTANCE AND CONFIGURATION: 3.1-mile loop

HIKING TIME: 2 hours

HIGHLIGHTS: Beautifully tended gardens with labeled plants and interpretive signs and varied sculpture and architecture

ELEVATION: 1,305' at trailhead, 1,399' at highest point

ACCESS: Open daily, sunrise–sunset; no fees or permits required

MAPS: USGS *Bentonville North*

FACILITIES: Restaurant and restrooms during museum hours

WHEELCHAIR ACCESS: The Art Trail and Crystal Bridges Trail are accessible.

COMMENTS: Leashed pets are allowed. Go to the Crystal Bridges website to reserve free tickets to tour the interior of the Frank Lloyd Wright house.

CONTACTS: Crystal Bridges Museum of American Art, 479-418-5700, crystalbridges.org

Overview

Imagine walking through an outdoor art museum that balances art, architecture, and nature without slighting one or the other. Then, imagine leaving the trail and entering a climate-controlled art museum with a restaurant and cold beverages. This is what you have with the Crystal Bridges trails! You'll want to make a full day of it so you can hike the trails described here and then visit the Crystal Bridges Museum for a meal and a free viewing of world-renowned art exhibits.

Route Details

Begin at the parking area next to the main entrance to the museum. Pause to have a look at the welded stainless steel tree sculpture titled *Yield*. Trail intersections have clear signs. There are no trail blaze markers. Follow the Orchard Trail for 0.2 mile, and then turn right onto the Tulip Tree Trail. You enter a lush hardwood forest with views of the museum down to your right. Stop and admire the Tulip Tree Shelter, originally built as a small-scale prototype to test the engineering of the museum's arched roof. The roofing was repurposed to form this shelter.

At 0.6 mile, you'll come to a small overlook giving you a view of the Bachman-Wilson House, built in 1954 by Frank Lloyd Wright. The structure was dismantled at its original location in New Jersey and relocated to this beautiful spot overlooking Crystal Springs. After the overlook, turn right onto Crystal Spring Trail. You'll do a short out-and-back across the spring and get a closer look at the Frank Lloyd Wright house.

Be sure to spend a few minutes at the spring and the small stone bridge that crosses over the source of the spring above a beautiful little cascade.

At 0.7 mile, turn southwest (left) onto the paved Art Trail. At 1.0 mile, restrooms are on the left of the trail. You'll arrive at a gate leading to the Compton Gardens, located at the home place of Neil Compton. Compton was the founder of the Ozark Society and

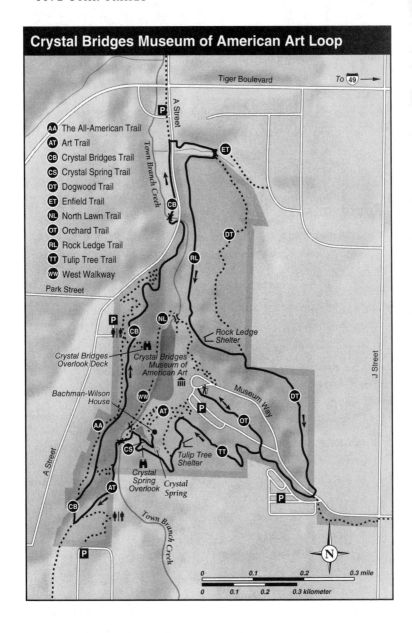

Crystal Bridges Museum of American Art Loop

- **AA** The All-American Trail
- **AT** Art Trail
- **CB** Crystal Bridges Trail
- **CS** Crystal Spring Trail
- **DT** Dogwood Trail
- **ET** Enfield Trail
- **NL** North Lawn Trail
- **OT** Orchard Trail
- **RL** Rock Ledge Trail
- **TT** Tulip Tree Trail
- **WW** West Walkway

Tiger Boulevard

To 49

A Street

Town Branch Creek

Park Street

Crystal Bridges Overlook Deck

Crystal Bridges Museum of American Art

Bachman-Wilson House

Rock Ledge Shelter

Museum Way

Tulip Tree Shelter

Crystal Spring Overlook

Crystal Spring

A Street

J Street

Town Branch Creek

N

0   0.1   0.2   0.3 mile

0   0.1   0.2   0.3 kilometer

instrumental in the saving of the Buffalo River. This would be a good area to explore if you have extra time. It is an out-and-back, but you're staying with the Crystal Bridges trails for this trip.

Turn right (north) onto the paved Crystal Bridges Trail. You'll see lots of side trails up on your left for mountain bikes. These are well-built trails including some fun bridges and winding paths. You're sharing the paved trails with cyclists too, so stay to the right and watch for bikes.

You'll come to an observation deck on the right at 1.3 miles. This stone structure was built as nature's response to the architecture of Crystal Bridges. The underlying philosophy at Crystal Bridges is that art and nature are essential to the human spirit and should be available to all, regardless of socioeconomic status. This is a beautiful location to let your spirit savor the beauty of art and nature. Trees close by are suitable for hanging a hammock. What a great place for a nap!

At 1.5 miles, you'll walk along a metal rail with a view of the West Lawn below. This is a good place to access the museum if you need to cut your walk short.

At 1.6 miles, you'll come to a collection of sandstone columns arranged next to the trail. This sculpture is titled *Where They Cried* and uses Boston Mountain native stone to reflect on the Trail of Tears.

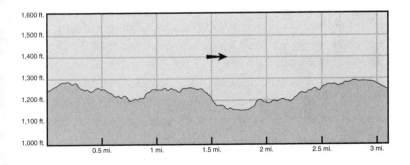

TRAILS PASS OVER SEVERAL BEAUTIFULLY BUILT BRIDGES.

Continue down the paved path and pass under the road and over a creek. At 1.8 miles, turn east (right) on Enfield Trail. You'll see a busy highway (Tiger Boulevard) up ahead. If you go underneath this busy highway, you'll know you missed your turn onto Enfield Trail.

At just after 1.9 miles, turn right onto the Dogwood/Rock Ledge Trail. Then take a right onto the Rock Ledge Trail. This trail follows the base of a ledge carved out for a 19th-century railroad that was never completed. You'll see redbud, cedar, and the West Lawn down on your right. Later, views of the Crystal Bridges Museum come into view down on the right.

At 2.25 miles, a spur trail goes down to Crystal Bridges on the right. Stay straight, crossing a stone bridge. At 2.3 miles, come to the Rock Ledge Shelter, a great spot for a break.

Turn right (south) onto Dogwood Trail at 2.4 miles. This puts us back on a paved trail. There are nice hardwoods on the right and a residential area on the left.

At 2.8 miles, the Dogwood Trail ends at a parking area. Take a right (northwest) onto Orchard Trail and follow it back to the museum entrance. There is parking, a shuttle service, and a Hydration Station if you want to purchase bottled water located at this intersection.

Watch traffic at the road crossing. You're now backtracking the first couple of tenths of your walk. When you arrive at the Crystal Bridges entrance, you've completed a 3.1-mile hike.

Nearby Attractions

Compton Gardens and Conference Center is the homesite of Dr. Neil Compton, founder of the Ozark Society. Dr. Compton was a leader in efforts to preserve the Buffalo National River (Peel Compton Foundation: 479-254-3870; peelcompton.org).

Northwest Arkansas Trails Razorback Greenways has developed a series of trails connecting the cities of Fayetteville, Springdale, Bentonville, and Rogers. These are open to foot traffic but ideal for biking. Maps are available at nwatrails.org.

Directions

The museum is located on Museum Way, off NE J Street in Bentonville, Arkansas. If you are entering Bentonville from I-49, take Exit 88 and go west on Central Avenue. Travel 0.3 mile and turn right onto John DeShields Boulevard. After you cross NE J Street, DeShields becomes Museum Way and leads you to the museum entrance and parking garage.

Hobbs State Park:
Pigeon Roost Loop

SCENERY: ★ ★ ★
TRAIL CONDITION: ★ ★ ★ ★ ★
CHILDREN: ★ ★ ★ ★
DIFFICULTY: ★ ★ ★
SOLITUDE: ★ ★ ★

FISHING IS POPULAR ON THE BEAVER LAKE INLET NEAR THE TRAIL.

GPS TRAILHEAD COORDINATES: N36° 17.427' W93° 55.850'

DISTANCE AND CONFIGURATION: 8.5-mile balloon

HIKING TIME: 6 hours

HIGHLIGHTS: Views of the Pigeon Roost arm of Beaver Lake, wonderful trail condition, variety of plants and wildlife

ELEVATION: 1,465' at trailhead, 1,465' at highest point, 1,176' at lowest point

ACCESS: Open 24/7; no fees or permits required

MAPS: USGS *War Eagle*

FACILITIES: Restroom at the trailhead

WHEELCHAIR ACCESS: No

COMMENTS: Leashed pets are allowed. A shorter option is to take the Dry Creek Trail to form a 4.2-mile hike. Trail brochures are available at the trailhead kiosk and Hobbs State Park Visitor Center.

CONTACTS: Hobbs State Park Conservation Area, 479-789-5000, arkansasstateparks.com/hobbsstateparkconservationarea

Overview

Pigeon Roost Trail is a delight to walk. Your feet, and lungs, will thank you. The tread and drainage throughout this trail are excellent. The hills are few and gradual. Tim Ernst, an Arkansas trail advocate, writer, and professional photographer, built this trail in 1990. The trail was named for the now-extinct passenger pigeons that roosted in this area during the 1800s.

The woods through which this trail passes support a wide variety of plants. You'll see beautiful ferns and open views across the forest floor in this mixed hardwood and pine forest. This is an excellent hike for birders and nature watchers.

Route Details

The Pigeon Roost Loop is made up of two trails, the Dry Creek Loop and Huckleberry Loop. A shorter hike option is the Dry Creek Loop at 4.2 miles. An old roadbed intersects the trail and cuts about 4 miles from the longer loop, a nice option for younger hikers. The trail itself is usually dry. Water is only available from Beaver Lake and must be filtered.

The trail begins 0.5 mile west of the Hobbs State Park Visitor Center at a large parking area on AR 12. You'll begin on a wide tread going slightly downhill. The trail is marked with 2-by-6-inch white blazes.

You'll come to a trail that turns to the south (left) at 0.7 mile. Take that trail and climb alongside of a small, usually dry, drainage. By turning left here and doing the loop clockwise, you'll enjoy the beautiful lake views at the end of your hike, making a nice climax for the day. After following the drainage a short distance, you'll cross it and begin climbing the other side on several crosstie steps.

At 1.9 miles, you'll arrive at the junction for the Dry Creek Loop Trail. You're going to continue straight and do the entire Pigeon Roost Loop for an 8.5-mile hike. If you choose to do the shorter Dry Creek Loop, you'll turn right and take the 0.5-mile walk

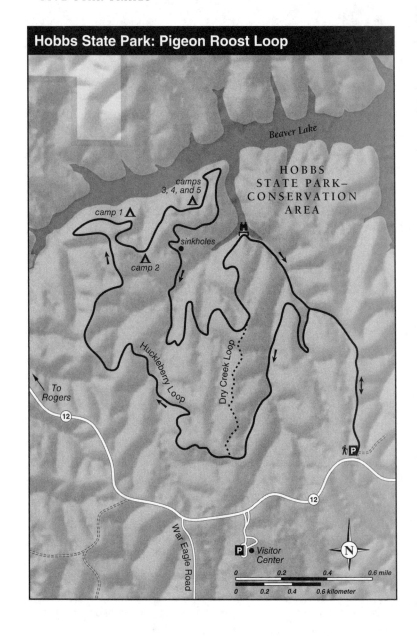

Hobbs State Park: Pigeon Roost Loop

Beaver Lake

HOBBS
STATE PARK–
CONSERVATION
AREA

camps
3, 4, and 5

camp 1

sinkholes

camp 2

Huckleberry Loop

Dry Creek Loop

To Rogers

12

12

War Eagle Road

P | Visitor Center

N

0   0.2   0.4   0.6 mile

0   0.2   0.4   0.6 kilometer

north leading to the next junction, where you'll reconnect with the Pigeon Roost Loop.

Continuing straight on the Huckleberry Loop, you'll take a nice walk in the woods passing several deep hollows and a few deep sink-holes on your left and right.

At 2.4 miles, you'll walk down to a low point into a dry creek bed. At 3.0 miles, you'll begin passing several deep hollows. Makes you wonder what type of erosion must have carved these hollows. Watch for sinkholes too.

At 3.9 miles, Beaver Lake comes into view down on your left. This is the Pigeon Roost Arm of Beaver Lake. At 4.2 miles, you get to a spur trail leading to campsite 1. Spur trails are marked with blue-painted blazes. There are five campsites, all positioned well off the trail and separated from each other by a good distance. Campsites have tent pads and metal fire ring grills. If you choose to do this trail as an overnighter, be sure you've registered at the Hobbs State Visitor Center.

At 4.9 miles, you'll follow a couple of switchbacks down to the lake level. If you need to filter some drinking water, a short trail branches off and takes you down to the water and then back to the main trail. As you continue down the trail, you'll pass a few sinkholes; some of them are very pronounced and easy to see.

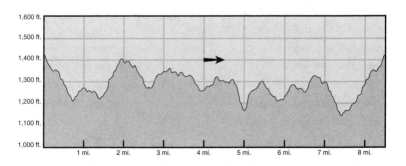

LUSH FERNS LINE SOME SECTIONS OF THE TRAIL.

At 6.0 miles, you'll follow a couple of switchbacks and a pretty good climb. This climb sticks out because it's one of the few huff-and-puff sections on this trail.

You'll come to an intersection of the Dry Creek Loop Trail coming in from your right at 6.8 miles. Turn left (north) here and continue on the Huckleberry Loop. There is a sign indicating that the trailhead is 1.5 miles away. As you walk, you'll see some views of the lake down on your left. You'll arrive at Pigeon Roost Arm of Beaver Lake Overlook at 7.3 miles. There is a bench, and you'll see some nice rock formations close to the water worthy of exploration. This is a great place to spend some time.

Continue on the trail, following an intermittent creek that flows into the lake. You'll cross a couple of small crosstie bridges. These are covered with wire fencing to give you traction. You'll pass some nice areas for wildflowers in spring and summer.

At 7.7 miles, you'll come to the initial trail that you started with heading to the southeast. The trail climbs slightly back to the trailhead for an 8.5-mile hike.

Nearby Attractions

Hobbs State Park Visitor Center is filled with interesting displays related to the area's history and geology. The wheelchair-accessible Ozark Plateau Trail begins at the visitor center (479-789-5000; arkansasstateparks.com/hobbsstateparkconservationarea).

War Eagle Mill is a beautiful stop for photographers and houses a restaurant. You may tour this working mill and purchase freshly ground grains (479-789-5343; wareaglemill.com).

Directions

Drive east out of Rogers on AR 12 for 13.0 miles. You'll pass the Hobbs State Park Visitor Center on your right. Continue driving east on AR 12 for 0.5 mile to the Pigeon Roost Trailhead on your left.

10

Glory Hole Falls

SCENERY: ★ ★ ★ ★ ★
TRAIL CONDITION: ★ ★ ★ ★
CHILDREN: ★ ★ ★ ★
DIFFICULTY: ★ ★ ★
SOLITUDE: ★ ★ ★

GLORY HOLE FALLS

GPS TRAILHEAD COORDINATES: N35° 49.702' W93° 23.427'

DISTANCE AND CONFIGURATION: 2-mile out-and-back

HIKING TIME: 1.5 hours

HIGHLIGHTS: Waterfall that flows through a hole in a thick rock house bluff

ELEVATION: 2,151' at trailhead, 2,151' at highest point

ACCESS: Open 24/7; no fees or permits required

MAPS: USGS *Fallsville*

FACILITIES: None

WHEELCHAIR ACCESS: No

COMMENTS: Good trail for kids and dogs. Hike to the falls in the early morning hours for the best photos and to avoid the crowds.

CONTACTS: Buffalo Outdoor Center, 870-861-5514, buffaloriver.com

Overview

This short hike takes you to a beautiful and unusual waterfall that flows through a hole in a wide bluff. The valley around the intermittent stream that flows through Glory Hole Falls is beautiful. This area gets a lot of use, so tread lightly.

Route Details

There are no trail markers on this unmaintained trail. Due to heavy use and the fact that part of the trail follows an old forest road, the route is clear. As of this writing, a small 8-by-10-inch sign with an arrow that says GLORY HOLE is visible from the highway.

Begin hiking at the highway, following a dirt road southeast through a level hardwoods area. If the falls are flowing, you're probably going to have a muddy walk. It's just one of the hazards of viewing waterfalls in Arkansas.

A little after 0.3 mile, veer to the right (southwest), leaving this roadbed, and descend on another dirt road that shortly switchbacks to the northwest as it continues downhill.

At 0.7 mile, you'll cross a small stream. You can gauge the flow of the falls by the level of this stream, but don't turn around if the flow is light. The Glory Hole is beautiful at all water levels. After crossing the stream, the road bends to the left.

The trail comes close to the creek and then crosses a small drain before proceeding downstream. Glory Hole comes into view down in the streambed on your left.

The waterfall and surrounding area are a treasure. Sadly, you may see some evidence of vandalism and scratching on rocks. Avoid doing anything that would further damage this beautiful area. The whole valley is worthy of exploration. If you attempt to view the waterfall from above, do so with caution.

Backtrack the way you came to complete this 2-mile hike.

Glory Hole Falls

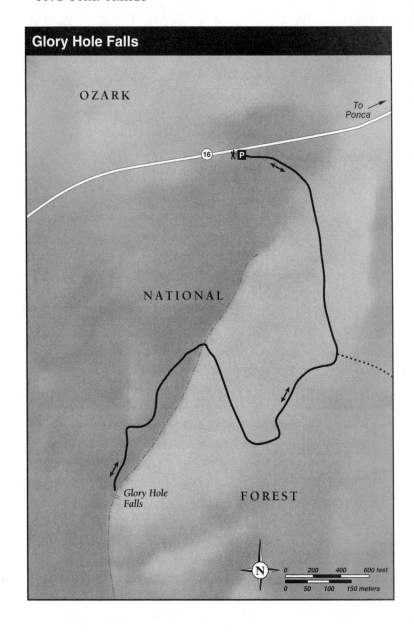

OZARK

To
Ponca

16 P

NATIONAL

Glory Hole
Falls

FOREST

N

| 0 | 200 | 400 | 600 feet |
| 0 | 50 | 100 | 150 meters |

Nearby Attractions

The Ponca Elk Education Center is filled with exhibits and resources about the Buffalo River area and elk population. It's a great side trip for young and old alike (870-861-2432; agfc.com/education/Pages /EducationCenterPonca.aspx).

The Buffalo Outdoor Center has sandwiches, ice cream, cabins, shuttles, and trail advice (870-861-5514; buffaloriver.com).

Boxley Baptist Church is a historic site and one of the most photographed buildings in the region (870-861-5612; boxleybaptist church.org).

Directions

From Ponca, drive southeast on AR 43 South 4.5 miles. Continue onto AR 21 South and drive 11.2 miles. Take a slight right onto AR 16 West/AR 21 South and drive 2.3 miles. Just before arriving at the trailhead, the road makes a sweeping turn to the left, and Cassville Church is on the right. Begin watching on the left (south) side of the road for a small parking area and a small sign that says GLORY HOLE. If you pass a barn on your right with a large E, you've gone too far. The total distance from Ponca to the Glory Hole Trailhead is about 18 miles.

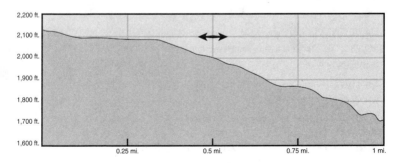

11

Whitaker Point–
Hawksbill Crag Trail

SCENERY: ★ ★ ★ ★ ★
TRAIL CONDITION: ★ ★ ★
CHILDREN: ★ ★ ★
DIFFICULTY: ★ ★
SOLITUDE: ★ ★

BALANCED ROCKS ON THE BLUFF EAST OF HAWKSBILL CRAG

GPS TRAILHEAD COORDINATES: N35° 53.894' W93° 27.479'

DISTANCE AND CONFIGURATION: 2.8-mile out-and-back

HIKING TIME: 2 hours

HIGHLIGHTS: Expansive view from Whitaker Point of Buffalo River and Whitaker Valley

ELEVATION: 2,179' at trailhead, 2,179' at highest point, 1,920' at lowest point

ACCESS: Open 24/7; no fees or permits required

MAPS: USGS *Boxley*

FACILITIES: None

WHEELCHAIR ACCESS: No

COMMENTS: Leashed pets are allowed. Good trail for kids if you keep an eye on them at blufflines.

CONTACTS: Buffalo Outdoor Center, 870-861-5514, buffaloriver.com

Overview

This short hike takes you to one of the most photographed scenes in Arkansas. Hawksbill Crag overlooks the Whitaker Creek drainage and is sometimes referred to as Whitaker Point. The whole trail is a visual treat, especially all along the blufflines, with several interesting rock formations and a small waterfall, not to mention the famous Hawksbill Crag.

Route Details

The trail begins at the gravel Cave Mountain Road opposite the wilderness access kiosk. The trail switchbacks downhill, following orange triangle and round-shaped markers. This trail receives a lot of use and is easy to follow through a mixed hardwood forest.

The trail continues downward and crosses a little stream at 0.9 mile. The trail then turns right and follows along this stream until it pours over the edge of the bluff. At this point, the trail turns left (southeast). You're now following along Whitaker Bluff with several viewing opportunities. Be cautious of your footing, and keep a close eye on your children.

At 1.2 miles, you see Hawksbill Crag protruding out over the edge. The trail leads right to Hawksbill Crag. This bluff is a great place for photos. Just be aware of where you're standing at all times. Hawksbill Crag is pretty wide, but from a distance, it appears as if you're much closer to the edge. Just don't get overconfident at its size. Over its edges are distant drops that would be fatal.

A lesser crag is just beyond Hawksbill. The stacked blocks of rock on this crag add another feature to the scene of the Whitaker and Buffalo River Valleys in the background.

After enjoying the scenery, begin working your way back to the trailhead, stopping to take in various views from the bluff.

Whitaker Point–Hawksbill Crag Trail

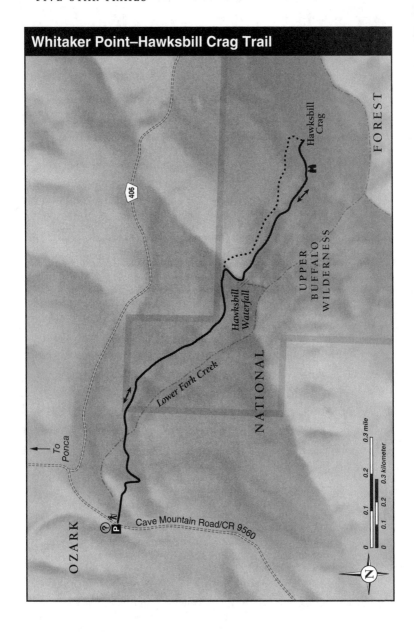

Nearby Attractions

The Ponca Elk Education Center is filled with exhibits and resources about the Buffalo River area and elk population. It's a great side trip for young and old alike (870-861-2432; agfc.com/education/Pages /EducationCenterPonca.aspx).

The Buffalo Outdoor Center has sandwiches, ice cream, cabins, shuttles, and trail advice (870-861-5514; buffaloriver.com).

Boxley Baptist Church is a historic site and one of the most photographed buildings in the region (870-861-5612; boxleybaptist church.org).

Directions

From the intersection of AR 43 and AR 74 in Ponca, drive southeast on AR 43 South 4.5 miles. Continue onto AR 21 South another 1.2 miles until you come to Cave Mountain Road on your right (west). If you cross the bridge over the Buffalo River, you've gone a few feet too far. Turn right onto Cave Mountain Road (County Road 9560). Drive 6.0 miles on the gravel road. After you pass the Cave Mountain Church on the right, the Whitaker Point Trailhead is only a short distance on your left. Parking is available at the wilderness access kiosk on the east side of the road. The trail begins on the east side of the road next to a large stone marker placed in recognition of Dale Bumpers.

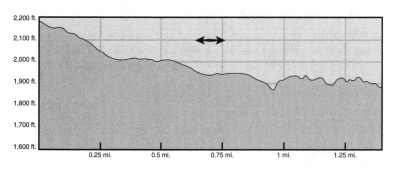

Smith Creek Preserve Trail

SCENERY: ★ ★ ★ ★ ★
TRAIL CONDITION: ★ ★ ★
CHILDREN: ★ ★ ★ ★
DIFFICULTY: ★ ★ ★ ★
SOLITUDE: ★ ★ ★

SMITH CREEK SPRING FLOWS FROM THE BASE OF A MOSS-COVERED HILLSIDE.

GPS TRAILHEAD COORDINATES: N35° 56.061' W93° 23.130'

DISTANCE AND CONFIGURATION: 5-mile balloon

HIKING TIME: 3 hours

HIGHLIGHTS: For a treat, begin this hike early and you'll hear a symphony of birdsong. Cascades in Smith Creek, Big Spring, and Elise Falls are just a few of the highlights to be seen.

ELEVATION: 1,676' at trailhead, 1,676' at highest point

ACCESS: Open 24/7; no fees or permits required

MAPS: USGS *Boxley Murray*

FACILITIES: None

WHEELCHAIR ACCESS: No

COMMENTS: Leashed pets are allowed.

CONTACTS: Arkansas Nature Conservancy, 501-663-6699, tinyurl.com/smithcreekpreserve

Overview

Judging from the strata making up the sedimentary bluffs bordering Smith Creek, there's nothing new about this area geologically, but public access to this beautiful location is new. Thanks to Marty and Elise Roenigk, who transferred their property to the Nature Conservancy in 2005 to establish Smith Creek Preserve, this area will be protected from development.

This is a new trail and a real jewel of Arkansas. After my first hike through, I said it was like Hurricane Creek on steroids. The Hurricane Creek Wilderness Area is a section on the Ozark Highlands Trail that involves at least two days of hiking to complete. Smith Creek has similar scenic qualities but condensed into a much smaller area, making it the ideal day hike.

Route Details

Pass the Smith Creek Trail kiosk then head through a gate and begin walking down a roadbed. At 0.1 mile, a trail to the left takes you to Elise Falls, but you'll visit the falls toward the end of your hike, coming out at this intersection to return to the trailhead. For now, head right.

This hike is mostly following old roadbeds. When the trail moves away from old roadbeds, watch for round yellow arrows indicating the trail. When the creek is flowing, you'll want to wear shoes you don't mind getting muddy. You might also want to carry water shoes for wading in the creek and for wet crossings if water is flowing strongly.

At 0.8 mile down the roadbed, you'll hear a small tributary that flows into Smith Creek. Then, at mile 1.0, veer right, cross a footbridge, and come to a picnic table and fire ring. Continuing straight on the trail, Smith Creek is on your left. You'll see some great views into the creek drainage as you walk upstream toward Big Spring.

You'll be following Smith Creek down to your left all the way to Big Spring at 1.9 miles. Several nice side trips down to the creek are indicated with yellow arrows so watch for these. These will increase your mileage a little, but they're worth the extra distance.

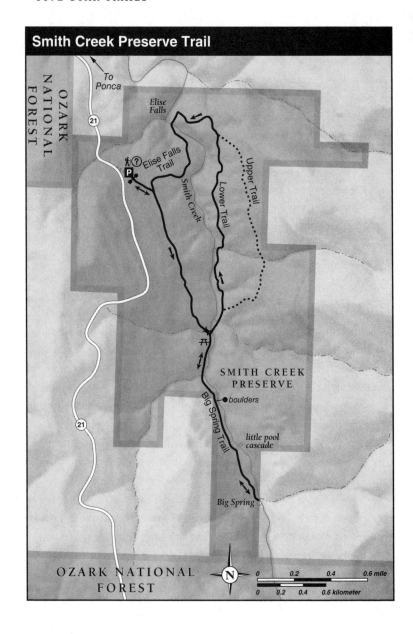

Smith Creek Preserve Trail

To Ponca

OZARK NATIONAL FOREST

21

Elise Falls

Elise Falls Trail

P

Smith Creek

Lower Trail

Upper Trail

21

SMITH CREEK PRESERVE

Big Spring Trail

boulders

little pool cascade

Big Spring

OZARK NATIONAL FOREST

N

| 0 | 0.2 | 0.4 | 0.6 mile |

| 0 | 0.2 | 0.4 | 0.6 kilometer |

You'll pass a small sinkhole on the right at mile 1.1, and then come to what might be a wet crossing. At 1.3 miles, a short spur leads east to a boulder area and cascade area of the creek. Each of the arrows you pass indicates a place you'll want to explore as you hike the out-and-back portion of this hike. You'll get two looks at everything, from the footbridge to Big Spring.

At about 1.6 miles, the Big Gem and Blue Hole areas are worth a stop and see. The Big Gem is a massive boulder in the middle of the creek.

Continue up Smith Creek and arrive at Big Spring at 1.9 miles. This is a large, moss-covered sprinkling of rocks with a high volume of water flowing out and into Smith Creek. Tread lightly in this area to avoid damaging the spring.

After enjoying Big Spring, turn around and head back 1 mile to the little bridge crossing. When you arrive back at the bridge with 3 miles under your belt, watch for the trail markers to turn right and cross Smith Creek. Watch closely in this section for yellow markers. You'll climb an old road steeply past some rockwork at 3.1 miles. Watch for the intersection of Lower and Upper Trail signs. You're going to follow the Lower Trail for this trip, so turn left.

You'll see some nice views of bluffs, pools, and boulders in the Smith Creek canyon. It's a wonderful place to explore. At 3.4 miles, the trail moves up to the next bench. It is a steep climb.

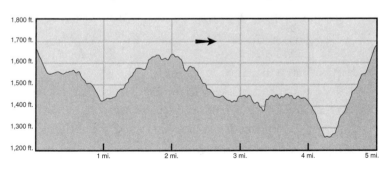

Once up to the next bench, the trail moves to the left (north). Watch for a trail marker closely in this section as you loosely follow an old roadbed, still following Smith Creek downstream but at a distance. This section of forest displays a nice hardwood canopy.

At 3.9 miles, you arrive at the Upper/Lower Trail junction. Continue through Shell Flats, and then turn left and begin descending back toward the creek drainage. After the hill bottoms out, turn toward the left and come to the Smith Creek drainage at 4.3 miles. You'll see a nice bluff on your left, and it appears that most of the water you saw earlier on Smith Creek is now flowing underground as it makes its way toward the Buffalo River. Water flow will be different depending on the season.

For an optional side trip, look to your right (northwest) for yellow arrows leading down the creek toward a tributary that leads to Elise Falls. This is some slick walking. Elise Falls is well worth the extra effort to see but does add about 0.2 mile to your overall hiking distance.

Back on the main trail at 4.3 miles, continue across the bluff area of Smith Creek and then down an old roadbed that soon begins to climb out of the creek drainage. It's a steep climb to the main trail. Arrive at the junction with the main trail at 4.8 miles and then turn right and go a short distance back to the trailhead to complete this 5-mile hike.

Nearby Attractions

The Ponca Elk Education Center is filled with exhibits and resources about the Buffalo River area and elk population. It's a great side trip for young and old alike (870-861-2432; agfc.com/education/Pages/EducationCenterPonca.aspx).

The Buffalo Outdoor Center has sandwiches, ice cream, cabins, shuttles, and trail advice (870-861-5514; buffaloriver.com).

Boxley Baptist Church is a historic site and one of the most photographed buildings in the region (870-861-5612; boxleybaptist church.org).

Directions

From the intersection of AR 43 and AR 74 in Ponca, drive southeast on AR 43 South 4.3 miles. Continue onto AR 21 South 0.6 mile and you'll pass Boxley Baptist Church on your right. Drive 2.6 miles past Boxley Baptist Church and watch for a small road to your left (east). This is the Smith Creek Preserve entrance. Drive down the short, steep hill to the trailhead.

CASCADES POUR AROUND LARGE BOULDERS NEXT TO BIG SPRING TRAIL.

13 # **Buffalo National River:**
Lost Valley Trail

SCENERY: ★ ★ ★ ★ ★
TRAIL CONDITION: ★ ★ ★ ★ ★
CHILDREN: ★ ★ ★ ★ ★
DIFFICULTY: ★ ★
SOLITUDE: ★ ★

NATURAL BRIDGE WATERFALL

GPS TRAILHEAD COORDINATES: N36° 00.623' W93° 22.513'

DISTANCE AND CONFIGURATION: 2.4-mile out-and-back with a little loop

HIKING TIME: 2 hours

HIGHLIGHTS: Eden Falls, natural bridge, and tall bluffs

ELEVATION: 1,115' at trailhead, 1,343' at highest point

ACCESS: Open 24/7; no fees or permits required

MAPS: USGS *Osage SW*; Trails Illustrated *Buffalo National River West Half*

FACILITIES: Pit toilets

WHEELCHAIR ACCESS: No

COMMENTS: No pets allowed. Good trail for children. As of this writing, camping at Lost Valley is closed to reduce environmental stress and because of flash flood concerns. This trail receives heavy use. If you want solitude, consider winter and early-morning hiking.

CONTACTS: Buffalo National River, 870-439-2502, nps.gov/buff; Buffalo Outdoor Center, 870-861-5514, buffaloriver.com

Overview

This short hike takes you through some of the most beautiful Buffalo River country in the state. You'll see towering bluffs, Eden Falls, Cob Cave, and a natural bridge. Lost Valley is a great trek for kids and novice hikers.

Route Details

Begin the trail walking through a forest of beech trees. The trail has a wide tread of crushed gravel with wooden borders. The trail follows along Clark Creek, which may appear to be dry even when Eden Falls is flowing. The water flows belowground, causing a surprising silence after being next to the running water earlier. During the wet season, the creek often flows strong with flash flooding, even damaging the area on rare occasions, but nothing like what the valley survived in October of 1960.

Lost Valley has a long history of impressing visitors. In 1946 the *St. Louis Globe-Democrat* did a full-page feature story on Lost Valley. Fourteen years later, in 1960, an event occurred that caused outrage among conservation-minded folks.

Lost Valley was under private ownership by Mrs. Harry Primrose, and she cherished the beauty of the valley. Her neighbors convinced her to spend a day in the nearby town of Jasper. As soon as she left, a local logger bulldozed a road through the valley and cut massive trees on either side. It was not unusual at the time for loggers to plunder trees without permission. This violent act on such a pristine forest increased levels of urgency for conservation efforts directed toward Lost Valley and the Buffalo River region in general. Neil Compton describes these events in his book, *The Battle for the Buffalo River.*

At 0.7 mile, you arrive at a junction with a trail that comes down from the hill on your left. You'll come back by this trail later in the hike. Turn right and arrive at the natural bridge at 0.8 mile. Note that the 1960 bulldozer scraped the hillside behind the bridge

Buffalo National River: Lost Valley Trail

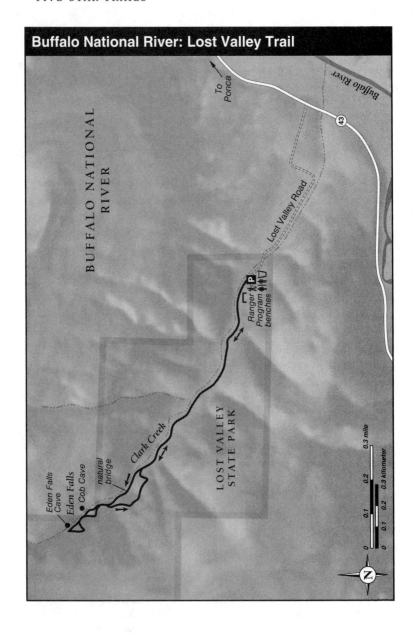

as it carved its way through the forest. Thankfully the wounds have healed, and this area is protected today.

You'll find a cascade flowing through the natural bridge and into a pool surrounded by large boulders and high bluffs. This is a great place to explore. You'll see soaring colorful bluffs typical of the Buffalo region stained with white, gray, and yellow features.

Follow stairs up the trail, watching on your left for deep-green mossy boulders and on your right for the massive Cob Cave, a large rock shelter. Corncobs from early inhabitants were found littering the area in and around this cave, protected from moisture by the overhanging rock. Kids enjoy calling out and hearing an echo.

Just past Cob Cave at 1.0 mile, you arrive at the base of Eden Falls, a beautiful 50-plus-foot waterfall flowing out of a small cave from above. There's also a waterfall inside the cave if you're up for some spelunking.

Follow stone and then concrete stairs up to the small entrance of the cave above Eden Falls at 1.2 miles. If you have two dependable sources of light and are prepared to get muddy, this little cave is worth some exploration. Water cascades through the cave and flows over Eden Falls. Deeper into the cave, a room opens up to a tall waterfall in the darkness. Watch for slick rocks.

Now backtrack on the trail down from the cave. At about 1.4 miles, you'll come to an intersection. Go straight, staying on the upper

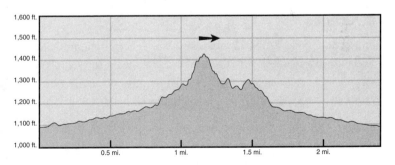

southwest side of the valley, following the signs back toward the trail-head. Looking across Clark Creek, you'll get a good view of the massive bluffs typical of the Buffalo region. Enjoy some easy walking in this section.

At 1.6 miles, the trail turns sharply left and down back to the original crushed-rock trail you hiked earlier. Backtrack to the trailhead to complete this 2.4-mile hike.

Nearby Attractions

The Ponca Elk Education Center is filled with exhibits and resources about the Buffalo River area and elk population. It's a great side trip for young and old alike (870-861-2432; agfc.com/education/Pages /EducationCenterPonca.aspx).

The Buffalo Outdoor Center has sandwiches, ice cream, cabins, shuttles, and trail advice (870-861-5514; buffaloriver.com).

Boxley Baptist Church is a historic site and one of the most photographed buildings in the region (870-861-5612; boxleybaptist church.org).

The Low Gap Cafe, located on AR 74 between Ponca and Jasper, serves up some seriously good food in this unlikely location. An outdoor dining deck overlooks the Steel Creek Valley to the northwest (870-861-5848; lowgapcafe.com).

Directions

From Ponca, follow AR 43 South for 1.3 miles. Turn right onto Lost Valley Road (County Road 1015). A sign indicates Lost Valley. You can see an elk viewing overlook just past the turnoff on AR 43. On Lost Valley Road, drive 0.5 mile to the trailhead.

Buffalo National River:
Centerpoint and Hemmed-In
Hollow Trails

SCENERY: ★ ★ ★ ★ ★
TRAIL CONDITION: ★ ★ ★ ★
CHILDREN: ★ ★
DIFFICULTY: ★ ★ ★ ★
SOLITUDE: ★ ★ ★

BUFFALO RIVER CLOSE TO SNEEDS CREEK

GPS TRAILHEAD COORDINATES: N36° 03.838' W93° 21.618'

DISTANCE AND CONFIGURATION: 11.7-mile out-and-back

HIKING TIME: 8 hours

HIGHLIGHTS: Visit one of the most expansive vistas over the Buffalo River and see the highest waterfall between the Appalachians and the Rocky Mountains.

ELEVATION: 2,261' at trailhead, 2,261' at highest point

ACCESS: Open 24/7; no fees or permits required

MAPS: USGS *Ponca;* Trails Illustrated *Buffalo National River West Half*

FACILITIES: None

WHEELCHAIR ACCESS: No

COMMENTS: No pets allowed. Hike to Big Bluff and back for a 6-mile out-and-back.

CONTACTS: Buffalo National River, 870-439-2502, nps.gov/buff; Buffalo Outdoor Center, 870-861-5514, buffaloriver.com

Buffalo National River: Centerpoint and Hemmed-In Hollow Trails

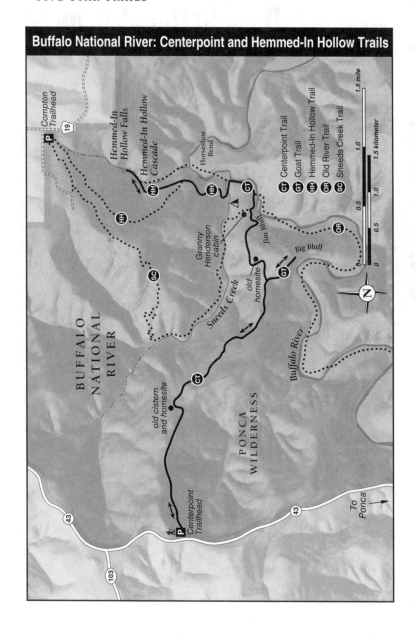

Overview

This is a demanding out-and-back hike with some constant climbing on the return route, but the rewards are well worth the effort. The hike includes majestic views from Big Bluff looking up the Buffalo River. You'll also visit the historical Granny Henderson cabin before dropping down to river level and eventually climbing to Hemmed-In Hollow, a 200-foot waterfall. Bring a water filter so you can stock up at Sneeds Creek before the tough climb back to the trailhead.

Route Details

Begin your hike at the Centerpoint Trailhead and parking area. The trail is crushed gravel in this section, following an old roadbed that goes all the way to the river. The road condition worsens as you descend toward the river.

Nice valley vistas come into view on the right just as you begin the hike. Some of the openings in the canopy here are courtesy of past ice storms that tend to do more damage up on the ridges.

At 0.6 mile, you'll notice fence rows and grassy, overgrown fields that are remnants of old homesteads. In springtime, you'll see lots of wildflowers in the open spots along this trail.

You'll pass an old homesite on the left at 1.2 miles. You might see remnants of an old cistern and spring. You'll begin to notice the

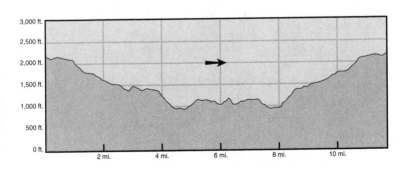

DAY HIKERS STAND IN AWE OF HEMMED-IN HOLLOW FALLS.

lay of the land sloping down on the left toward Sneeds Creek drainage. At 1.8 miles, the trail turns sharply toward the north.

At 2.4 miles, you'll catch glimpses of Buffalo River bluffs on your right when trees are leafless, and you may see portions of Big Bluff to the southeast. Shortly, you'll come to the Goat Trail at 2.7 miles. Turn right (south) and follow this primitive and unmaintained route. Hike with care because these bluffs are several hundred feet tall. This is a wonderful place for the geologically inclined. The sedimentary rock layers here line up with rock layers several hundred feet below at Jim Bluff next to the Buffalo River, attesting to the work of geologic changes over time.

From Big Bluff, you'll see the metal roof of one of the Villines homesteads down below. Many gnarly cedars grow along this bluff. Some are probably hundreds of years old and have survived in the thin soil here, sculpted by years of wind.

After taking in the views, head back to the main trail and continue hiking downhill to the east.

At 3.7 miles, you'll pass an old homesite on the right. Flowering bulbs in springtime and a stone foundation and stepstones alert you to the location. Rock walls, as well as some old barbed wire fencing, line the trail.

You may get a glimpse of a tin roof at 4.2 miles. This is the Granny Henderson cabin. Turn left (north) at the intersection and explore this historical area, but leave it undisturbed. Eva Barnes Henderson, known as Granny Henderson, left this home in 1978 and moved "up on the hill" to live with a daughter. Granny Henderson, who never learned to drive, said, "I've been lonesome out here sometimes, but I've never been afraid. I've always had me a mighty good dog and some good guns."

At 4.4 miles, you'll come to an intersection with Old River Trail (a horse trail). Go left and follow alongside the river, off in the distance on your right. The Old River Trail, marked with yellow blazes, is more appealing if you're on a horse. The trail eventually comes alongside the Buffalo River, arriving at Sneeds Creek, which may be a wet crossing.

At 4.6 miles, the horse trail (yellow blazes) continues across Sneeds and along the river. Turn left (west) at Sneeds Creek and go a couple hundred yards upstream, passing a campsite before crossing Sneeds Creek. Watch for the trail on the other side, and cross Sneeds Creek. This is usually excellent water for filtering if you're getting low.

After Sneeds Creek, the trail climbs up and out through a mossy little bluffline. At 5.2 miles, the trail passes through a concrete-looking bluffline with easy steps up to follow along the top, littered with gnarly cedar. If it's floating season, you may hear enthusiastic shouts from the river.

At 5.5 miles, you'll come to an intersection and go right toward the falls. Left will take you to Compton Trailhead, a shorter route to Hemmed-In Hollow, but it lacks the views of Big Bluff and the historical interests of Granny Henderson's cabin.

The magic begins pretty quickly as the blufflines come into view as you proceed along this route. You'll see several water features and small waterfalls in the Hemmed-In Hollow drainage, each worthy of exploration. Each of these would be special, but they're overshadowed by the 200-foot-plus falls coming up. At 6 miles, you come to the base of Hemmed-In Hollow Falls. The falls are 209 feet tall and beautiful, regardless of water levels.

After spending some time taking in the views of Hemmed-In Hollow, return to the Centerpoint Trailhead the way you came in. Be sure to check your water supply before passing Sneeds Creek on your way out. The continuous climb to Centerpoint can humble even the strongest of athletes.

As you arrive at Centerpoint, you will have completed an 11.8-mile hike. Mileage will be a little longer if you take the Goat Trail spur again on your hike out. It might be something you want to do if you're still feeling strong and want to see the bluff in late afternoon or evening light.

Nearby Attractions

Lost Valley Canoe is on the north end of Ponca and includes a campground with no RV hookups, a duplex bunkhouse, and a restroom with showers. It rents canoes and has a small convenience store (870-861-5522; lostvalleycanoe.com).

The Buffalo Outdoor Center has sandwiches, ice cream, cabins, shuttles, and trail advice (870-861-5514; buffaloriver.com).

The Low Gap Cafe, located on AR 74 between Ponca and Jasper, serves up some seriously good food in this unlikely location. An outdoor dining deck overlooks the Steel Creek Valley to the northwest (870-861-5848; lowgapcafe.com).

A FAMILY ENJOYS LUNCH AT BIG BLUFF OVERLOOKING THE BUFFALO RIVER.

Directions

From Ponca, take AR 43 northwest 3.3 miles. The trailhead and parking area will be on the right (east) side of the highway.

Round Top Mountain Loop

NORTH SCENIC POINT VISTA

GPS TRAILHEAD COORDINATES: N35° 59.038' W93° 10.713'

DISTANCE AND CONFIGURATION: 3.6-mile multiloop

HIKING TIME: 2.5 hours

HIGHLIGHTS: Expansive views from the South Gap and North Scenic Points, unusual rock formations and bluffs, rich environment for birds, and commemorative plaque for the crew of a B-25 that crashed into the mountain in 1948

ELEVATION: 1,668' at trailhead, 2,015' at highest point

ACCESS: Open 24/7; no fees or permits required

MAPS: USGS *Parthenon*

FACILITIES: Restrooms at the trailhead

WHEELCHAIR ACCESS: None on the hiking trail. A wheelchair-accessible paved path extends from the trailhead to an overlook. This sidewalk is not part of the hiking trail.

COMMENTS: Leashed pets are allowed. For a shorter hike, the lower Loop Trail gives you a 2-mile hike.

CONTACTS: Newton County Arkansas Chamber of Commerce, 870-446-2455, theozarkmountains.com

Overview

Round Top is one of those rare trails not requiring dirt road driving to access but providing wide vistas from two bluff-top overlooks. Hike Round Top Mountain, taking in the views of Jasper then admiring the bell-shaped mountain you just traveled, and then have a meal across the street from the historic Newton County Courthouse.

For history buffs, a commemorative plaque placed at the 1948 B-25 crash site fills the bill. Viewing Round Top Mountain from a distance, it's easy to imagine how a plane might crash there on a freezing, foggy night.

Route Details

You're going to like every step of this trail because each section offers something special. Climb quickly up the side of the mountain on several switchbacks. The well-built stairs at the beginning of the trail are representative of what you'll see throughout this hike anytime the going gets steep.

The switchbacks top out at 0.2 mile, and you're facing a large, white bluff. Turn right (north) and begin following this bench with the bluffline on your left. This is pleasant walking.

Watch for little tin nameplates on trees. You'll see quite a variety of hardwood species with a few pines and cedars at the upper elevations. Rustic wooden benches are placed along the trail.

There were no trail markers at this writing, but the tread is easy to follow.

Just after 0.4 mile, start watching on the left for the memorial marker commemorating pilots who died in the 1948 crash of a B-25 during a training mission. A small assortment of debris from the crash might be found next to the marker.

Shortly after the crash site, several large, light-colored boulders have tumbled away from the bluff, illustrating the recent effects of erosion from water, ice, plants, and time.

Round Top Mountain Loop

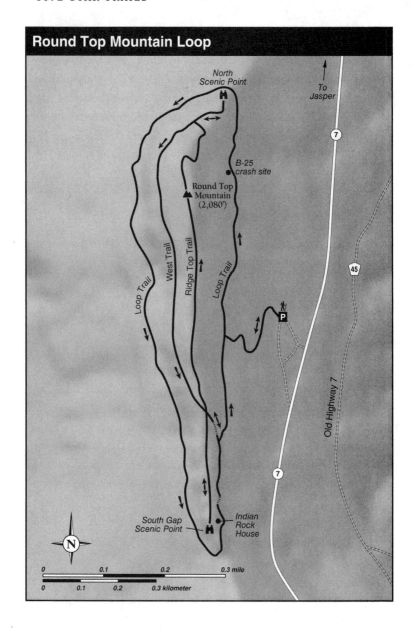

North
Scenic Point

To
Jasper

7

B-25
crash site

Round Top
Mountain
(2,080')

West Trail

Ridge Top Trail

Loop Trail

Loop Trail

Loop Trail

45

P

Old Highway 7

7

South Gap
Scenic Point

Indian
Rock
House

N

0	0.1	0.2	0.3 mile
0	0.1	0.2	0.3 kilometer

At 1.4 miles, turn left (east) and up over South Gap Pass, then follow the trail bearing left (north) with the bluff still on your left. After a short distance, you'll come to a rock outcrop that locals call Indian Rock House, a small covered bluff. Past the rock house, you'll pass between big boulders and down stairs complete with a wooden handrail.

Just past 1.6 miles, you'll arrive at a trail intersection. Follow the trail straight and along the bluff, climbing stairs to the next bench. An optional shorter hike can be completed from here if you veer right and down toward the trailhead instead of climbing the stairs to the next bench.

As you arrive on the upper bench, you'll come to a four-way intersection. Stay to the right on Ridge Top Trail. You'll take the Ridge Top Trail to North Scenic Point before returning to this point via the West Trail. You'll then hike out to the South Gap Scenic Point.

Now on to the Ridge Top Trail. There are big views off to the east with views both east and west opening up during fall and winter, when the trees lose their leaves. As you continue, the ridge becomes more pronounced. The trail climbs slightly toward Round Top and passes through lots of undergrowth and greenbriers due to the limited tree canopy overhead. If the going is easy here, say a word of thanks for trail maintainers.

At 2.0 miles, you come to Round Top at 2,080 feet. At 2.1 miles, descend slightly along the east side of the mountain. At 2.2 miles, turn

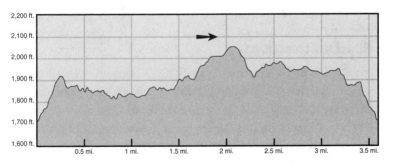

right onto a spur trail. You will arrive at the North Scenic Point at 2.3 miles. The views are fantastic. This is a great spot for lunch or a break.

Now backtrack the short distance back up to the West Trail intersection and continue around the west side of the mountain. Early on the West Trail looking to the northwest, you might spot the Little Buffalo River down below as it flows through the town of Jasper. You're now walking above the bluffs you viewed while hiking the Loop Trail.

The West Trail is a well-built tread on a fairly steep pitch. Watch your foot placement because a short slide down the hillside might put you at the edge of a bluff below.

Just before 2.9 miles, you'll come back to the four-way intersection. Veer right to the South Gap Scenic Point. Walking along this ridge, you'll enjoy views to the east and west. You'll see more pine and cedar on this ridge.

At 3.0 miles, you'll arrive at the South Gap Scenic Point. You're on top of those amazing rock bluffs you passed just before the Indian Rock House on the Loop Trail earlier. Be careful beyond the cedar fence. You'll hate to leave this spot knowing the hike is close to its end.

Backtrack to the four-way intersection. At 3.2 miles, take a sharp right and down the way you came toward the Loop Trail. At the bottom intersection, take a sharp left (north) back onto the Loop Trail.

At 3.4 miles, take a right and down to the trailhead to complete this 3.6-mile hike.

Nearby Attractions

The Ozark Cafe is a longtime landmark in the community. It is decorated with local historical photos, a whiskey still, and a stage for occasional live music (870-446-2976; ozarkcafe.com).

The Arkansas House Boardwalk Café is just one block from the square. You can rent rooms and enjoy good food at this location. Be sure to ask about the history of the watermill wheel out front (870-446-5900; arkansashouse.net).

ROCK FORMATIONS AT THE SOUTH SCENIC POINT

Directions

From the Newton County Courthouse on the square in Jasper, drive south on AR 7 2.4 miles. Watch for the ROUND TOP MOUNTAIN sign on the right.

Pedestal Rocks
Scenic Area

SCENERY: ★ ★ ★ ★ ★
TRAIL CONDITION: ★ ★ ★ ★ ★
CHILDREN: ★ ★ ★
DIFFICULTY: ★ ★ ★
SOLITUDE: ★ ★ ★

THIS MASSIVE PEDESTAL STANDS BELOW THE BLUFF-EDGED TRAIL.

GPS TRAILHEAD COORDINATES: N35° 43.413' W93° 00.911'

DISTANCE AND CONFIGURATION: 4-mile figure eight

HIKING TIME: 3 hours

HIGHLIGHTS: Some of Arkansas's most unusual pedestal rock formations, beautiful bluffs, expansive vistas, and Kings Bluff Falls

ELEVATION: 1,868' at trailhead, 1,890' at highest point

ACCESS: Open 24/7; no fees or permits required

MAPS: USGS *Sand Gap*

FACILITIES: Pit toilet and picnic table

WHEELCHAIR ACCESS: No

COMMENTS: Leashed pets are allowed. The first mile of this hike as an out-and-back is a less strenuous option for a 2-mile trip.

CONTACTS: Hankins Country Store, 870-294-5151

Overview

This hike packs a load of beauty into just under 4 miles. The Pedestal Rocks Scenic Area is a special place and a must-see destination in the Arkansas Ozarks. You'll see the sculpting of water over time as you view pedestals, arches, and towering bluffs from the trail. Be sure to bring your camera, but don't be surprised if your lens isn't wide enough to capture the size of some of the pedestals from top to bottom.

Route Details

The trailhead is located in a circle drive next to AR 16. There are no blazes on this trail, but the route is clear.

Begin by walking across a stone bridge and then veering to your left. The trail that comes in from the right is Kings Bluff Loop, but that is where you'll end your hike coming out.

At 0.1 mile, go straight at this intersection with the sign indicating Pedestal Rocks straight. Right takes you to Kings Bluff, but you'll add that loop after Pedestal Rocks Loop, hiking a figure eight. The trail to the left is where you'll come out after hiking Pedestal Rocks Loop.

This is a well-built trail following an old roadbed with drainage cuts to avoid washouts. You'll see some nice stone steps along this section as you gradually descend toward the bluffs with a few slight climbs along the way. This first stretch gives you a nice warm-up hike before reaching the scenic areas.

At 0.4 mile, you enter a pine grove with a few hardwoods mixed in. You'll hike past a warning sign stating to watch your children along this high bluff area.

At mile 1.0 you come to a sharp switchback to the left. You'll begin seeing the valley down to the right. You'll pass by a small spur route down to the bluff, but be patient and you'll come to a switchback that takes you down to the top of the bluff using a better route. Take some time to explore along the bluffline. Hiking to this point is

Pedestal Rocks Scenic Area

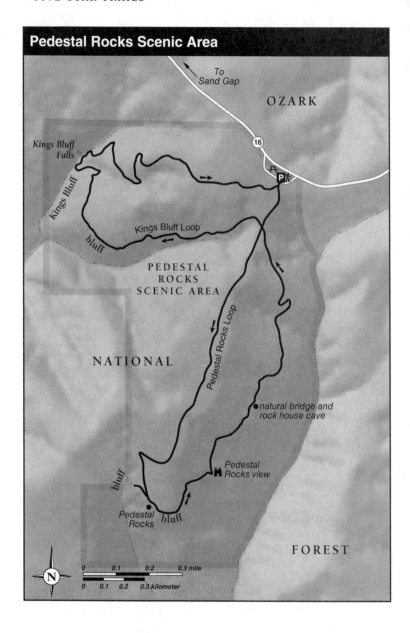

To
Sand Gap

OZARK

16

P

Kings Bluff
Falls

Kings Bluff

bluff

Kings Bluff Loop

PEDESTAL
ROCKS
SCENIC AREA

Pedestal Rocks Loop

NATIONAL

natural bridge and
rock house cave

Pedestal
Rocks view

bluff

Pedestal
Rocks

bluff

FOREST

N

| 0 | 0.1 | 0.2 | 0.3 mile |

| 0 | 0.1 | 0.2 | 0.3 kilometer |

a good out-and-back if you have limited time but want to see a good example of a pedestal rock.

Back on the main trail, continue around the bluffline, taking in views with every step. At 1.7 miles, you come to a natural bridge and small cave just east of the trail. This is a great area to explore. If you follow the little rock house cave to its far end, it comes to a drop-off, so be careful. This is a special place!

At 1.9 miles, the trail passes over a couple of small seasonal waterfalls. At mile 2.0, you'll move away from the bluffline and begin a gradual climb up switchbacks before coming to the intersection with Kings Bluff Trail at 2.5 miles. Going straight through this inter-section puts us on the Kings Bluff Loop going clockwise.

You're hiking through boulder-peppered fields with beautiful lichen-covered rocks. At 2.9 miles, expansive views open up all along the bluffline down to your left. Take this section slowly and enjoy the views. The enormous Kings Bluff begins to come into view at 3.2 miles. You'll arrive at Kings Bluff at 3.3 miles. This is a great spot to spend some time with your camera. Kings Bluff Falls is at the far end of the bluff.

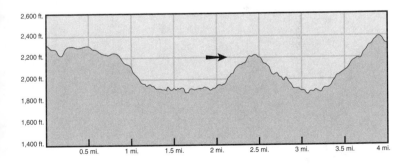

The trail moves away from Kings Bluff uphill on an old road-bed, first south, then veering east. This is a pretty steady climb and brings you up to the short spur where you'll turn left and head back to the trailhead to complete this 4-mile hike.

Nearby Attractions

Hankins Country Store is a treat to visit. You'll see lots of history on the walls, and it has great sandwiches (870-294-5151).

Hagarville Grocery, 30 miles west of Pelsor on AR 123, runs shuttles for hikers and is a popular resupply location for the Ozark Highlands Trail (479-885-6330).

Directions

From I-40 in Russellville, take Exit 81, AR Scenic Highway 7 (AR 7) north 35 miles to Sand Gap. Turn right (east) on AR 16 and drive 5.8 miles. Watch for a PEDESTAL ROCKS sign and entrance on the right.

Buffalo National River:
River View and Spring Hollow Trails

SCENERY: ★ ★ ★ ★ ★
TRAIL CONDITION: ★ ★ ★ ★
CHILDREN: ★ ★ ★ ★
DIFFICULTY: ★ ★ ★
SOLITUDE: ★ ★ ★

VIEW OF THE BUFFALO RIVER FROM A TRAILSIDE BUFF

GPS TRAILHEAD COORDINATES: N35° 59.171' W92° 45.824'

DISTANCE AND CONFIGURATION: 3.1-mile loop

HIKING TIME: 2 hours

HIGHLIGHTS: Views of the Buffalo River from a high bluffline and a visit to Collier Homestead, which dates back to 1928

ELEVATION: 672' at trailhead, 880' at highest point

ACCESS: Open 24/7; no fees or permits required

MAPS: USGS *Snowball* and *Marshall*

FACILITIES: Visitor center with restrooms, campgrounds, and Buffalo River access

WHEELCHAIR ACCESS: No, with the exception of the Collier Homestead from Searcy County Road 241 to the Buffalo River overlook. A wheelchair-accessible deck is located behind the Tyler Bend Visitor Center.

COMMENTS: No pets allowed on these trails. The short 0.5-mile walk from Collier Homestead to the Buffalo River overlook deck is an easy alternate hike.

CONTACTS: Buffalo National River, 870-439-2502, nps.gov/buff

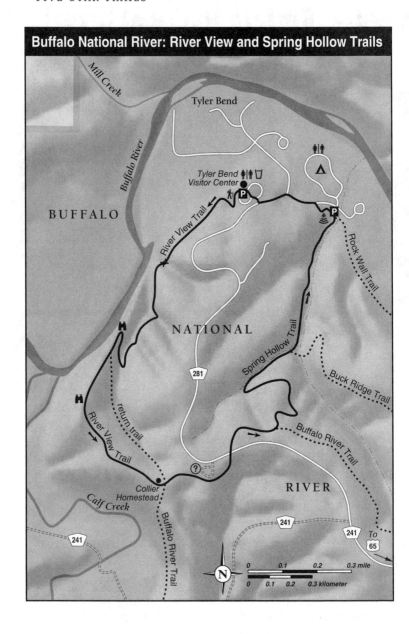

Buffalo National River: River View and Spring Hollow Trails

Overview

This combination of two Tyler Bend trails will give you expansive views of the Buffalo River and an intimate look into the lives of the resourceful people who settled this rough landscape.

This loop route also follows a short portion of the Buffalo River Trail that connects to the Ozark Highlands Trail to form a 200-plus-mile hiking trail as of this writing. The Buffalo River Trail will eventually become part of a 500-plus-mile trail from northwest Arkansas to Saint Louis, Missouri.

Route Details

There are several loop trail possibilities at Tyler Bend. This hike covers the most scenic and my personal favorite. Begin at the trailhead next to the visitor center. Descend into the woods, going left and then down a couple of switchbacks through mixed hardwood forest. There are no blazes, but the route is clear with marked intersections. Hiking counterclockwise presents some climbs early in the hike but downhills later when you're tired.

The trail comes to a nice set of wooden steps and a bridge that crosses a small creek bed. You'll then come to the edge of a hayfield visible through the undergrowth. You may hear the sound of the Buffalo River through the trees, as you're pretty close to water level down

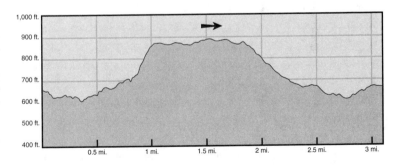

on your right. You'll come to a sign that indicates this trail leads to some high bluff tops and to be cautious.

After the bridge, the trail follows an intermittent streambed below on your right. At 0.7 mile, cross the little streambed you've been following. Then head up the opposite side of the stream, climbing slightly to a beautiful overlook at 0.8 mile on the edge of a tall bluff.

After enjoying the overlook, continue walking along this bluff-line with views into the Buffalo River Valley below. At 0.9 mile, come to a sign indicating a return trail on your left. This route would make this a short loop, returning you to this intersection, but for today's hike, continue straight, following the bluffline and climbing steeply.

A reminder: limestone can be very slick when wet or worn smooth by passing feet. It doesn't have to look slick to be slick.

At 1.0 mile, top out this climb to a wooden deck overlook on your right. This is a beautiful spot for a rest and some photos.

Continuing past the overlook, follow a wide, flat trail, heading southeast to the Collier Homestead. You're walking through the large garden plot where Sod Collier and his wife, Ida Mae, used to grow enough to support their family through even the harshest winters. In 1928, the Colliers traveled from Kentucky to Arkansas in a truck to claim this remnant of land still available for homesteading.

Continue to the front of the homesite and turn left (east), following the wide trail to the trailhead, passing a turnoff to the return trail that intersects with the trail you were on earlier. Continue straight to County Road 281 at 1.5 miles and turn right at the Collier Homestead kiosk. Look right for a small sign pointing into a cedar grove and follow the trail a short distance, continuing across CR 281. This small portion of the Buffalo River Trail will lead you to the Spring Hollow Trail. At 1.9 miles, arrive at the Spring Hollow Trail junction, turn left (northwest), and begin hiking toward the visitor center.

The Spring Hollow Trail takes you through a dense hardwood forest forming a thick canopy and shade, resulting in an open under-story and less undergrowth. This trail is a treat. The first time I hiked this trail, I hoped Spring Hollow would be true to its name since I was running low on water. I was in luck and filtered some wonderful water from one of the small streams in the hollow at 2.2 miles.

The trail follows this drainage awhile. After about 100 yards, the stream disappears underground before reemerging 50 yards later.

At 2.4 miles, cross the small drainage you've been following again and come to an intersection for the Buck Ridge Trail. Buck Ridge Trail veers right, but stay left on Spring Hollow Trail, following the hollow that is now deeper.

You'll come out of the woods at 2.8 miles with the park amphitheater on your left. The amphitheater is an alternative trailhead and would be convenient for campers. Turn left in front of the amphitheater and cross a small parking lot to the road. The campgrounds and restrooms are across the road. Turn left (west) and follow the road uphill to a stop sign; turn left again onto CR 281. Walk along this road on the left side, so you'll see oncoming traffic. Cross the road carefully into the visitor center parking lot to complete this 3.1-mile hike.

Nearby Attractions

St. Joe (stjoearkansas.org), a historical town, is on AR 65 northwest of Tyler Bend. St. Joe is home of the Historic Missouri and North Arkansas Railroad Depot and Museum.

Directions

From Marshall, Arkansas, drive US 65 North 9.5 miles. Turn left on Searcy County Road 241. You'll pass the Collier Homestead Trailhead on your left that leads to a short wheelchair-accessible trail to the historical site and a Buffalo River overlook. CR 241 becomes CR 281. For the longer loop hike described here, continue on the main road 2.3 miles to the Tyler Bend Visitor Center. Turn left into the visitor center parking lot. The trailhead is at the parking area on the left side of the visitor center.

From Harrison, drive 31 miles south on US 65, arriving at Searcy CR 241, the entrance to Tyler Bend.

Buffalo National River:
Indian Rockhouse Trail

SCENERY: ★ ★ ★ ★ ★
TRAIL CONDITION: ★ ★ ★ ★
CHILDREN: ★ ★ ★ ★
DIFFICULTY: ★ ★ ★
SOLITUDE: ★ ★ ★

VIEW FROM INSIDE THE INDIAN ROCKHOUSE

GPS TRAILHEAD COORDINATES: N36° 04.871' W92° 34.154'

DISTANCE AND CONFIGURATION: 3.5-mile balloon

HIKING TIME: 2.5 hours

HIGHLIGHTS: Indian Rockhouse with a flowing spring in the back of the cave. You'll see a waterfall, beautiful rocky creek, several sinkholes, and smaller caves.

ELEVATION: 888' at trailhead, 925' at highest point

ACCESS: Open 24/7; no fees or permits required

MAPS: USGS *Cozahome;* Trails Illustrated *Buffalo River East Half;* map and description flier available in the Buffalo Point Ranger Station

FACILITIES: Restrooms available at the ranger station. Buffalo Point has walk-in campgrounds, as well as RV sites and cabins.

WHEELCHAIR ACCESS: No

COMMENTS: No pets allowed. A trail brochure is available in the visitor center.

CONTACTS: Buffalo National River, Buffalo Point Ranger Station, 870-449-4311, nps.gov/buff

Overview

This trail includes a dose of history, archaeology, and some beautiful sights too. Indian Rockhouse is a fascinating place to explore. This trail includes waterfalls, sinkholes, caves, a prospecting mine, and a natural bathtub. There's something to see every step of the way on this hike. Just be sure you bring drinking water and energy for the hike out at the end.

Route Details

The trail begins across County Road 268 from the parking area and kiosk. Watch for traffic as you cross. You'll begin walking northwest down a broad roadbed. Stay to the right on the lower trail. The hike ends on the trail approaching the trailhead from alongside the highway.

This trail has a wide tread as it follows a well-built old roadbed. These woods are mostly hardwood with a few pine mixed in. You'll come quickly to a sign that indicates to turn right to the northeast. This is not an intersection.

At 0.3 mile, you'll come to a large sinkhole. At times, you might see steam coming from this sinkhole. At 0.5 mile, walk over to the edge of a steep drainage, and, to the left, you might hear a waterfall below. A short spur trail to the left takes you to the top of the waterfall, but you'll see it from below later.

Follow the trail downhill and eventually down spiraling stairs. You'll pass more sinkholes. Be sure to notice the sinkhole that is round and deep green with moss-covered rock. The trail curves left into a valley, arriving at a waterfall at 0.6 mile.

After passing the base of the waterfall, the trail leads back downstream away from the waterfall at a fairly steep pitch. At 0.75 mile, you'll reach an old prospecting zinc mine. This mine is approximately 8 miles as the crow flies from the Rush mining community. No zinc was found in this prospect hole, probably dug in the 1880s. Continue past the "zincless" mine, heading downhill at a steep descent. Look for some tough climbs later in this hike as payback.

Buffalo National River: Indian Rockhouse Trail

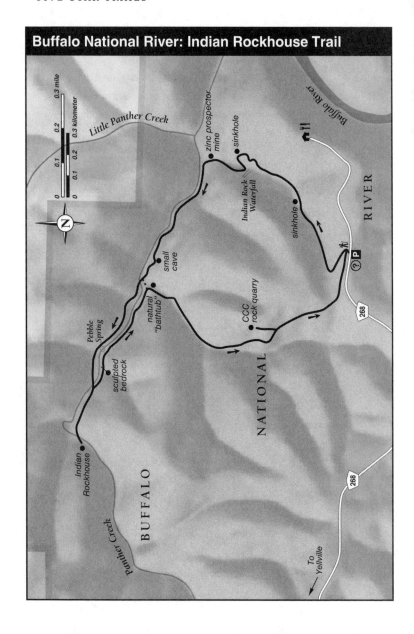

At 0.8 mile, you'll approach Panther Creek and enjoy a beautiful walk alongside the creek with nice bluffs on both sides. It was fairly dry the first time I hiked it in springtime following some rain a few weeks earlier. My guess is that during drier seasons, this creek would be bone-dry. There were some pockets of water, and it was good to filter, but don't count on water in fall or summer.

At 1.2 miles, the trail swings up and away from the creek toward a boulder area with a small cave. Just after the little cave, at 1.3 miles, the trail intersects with a paved path (don't take it). Stay to the right across the creek and continue walking toward the Indian Rockhouse. Up to your left, a small branch flows into Panther Creek. You'll see this intersection again on your return path when you turn and head up this creek. Pretty quickly you're hiking above Panther Creek, following a roadbed. You may see the return trail on the other side of the creek bed.

You'll come to a wide, flat rock crossing the trail and a nice slot in the creek just to the left of the trail in the Panther Creek drainage. This area is usually wet and very slick for several yards. Just after this flat rock across the trail, you'll come to a Panther Creek crossing at 1.7 miles, beginning the spur trail to Indian Rockhouse, climbing high above Panther Creek down on your right. The trail then quickly comes downhill back to Panther Creek, where you cross and enter a

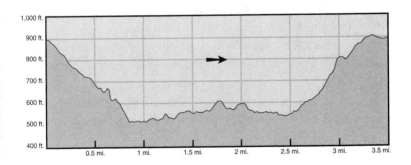

CHILDREN EXPLORE THE FLOOR OF INDIAN ROCKHOUSE.

beautiful canyon area. You may hear running water from the spring in the back of Indian Rockhouse.

Arrive at the Indian Rockhouse Cave at 1.9 miles. Stalagmites on the floor of the cave were formed by years of mineral deposits from the dripping ceiling. The cave has many slick spots, so be careful. A clear spring flows in the back of the cave.

After spending some time in the cave, backtrack to the earlier creek intersection at 2.1 miles. After you cross Panther Creek, a sign indicates RETURN TRAIL. The trail climbs, and Panther Creek is now down to your left. Cross a small bridge. Right after the bridge, you'll come alongside the sculpted bedrock that includes a small slot in the creek. This is a neat area to see. The trail moves away and then comes to Pebble Spring, another area to explore.

At 2.5 miles, a sign indicates a trailhead to the right. Turn right and climb a little side creek that feeds into the natural "bathtub." This actually looks like a nice little round bathtub with a small cascade feeding the bowl. Get psyched for a continuous climb. You're making up the elevation for all the downhills at the beginning of the hike. Pretty quickly, the trail crosses the drainage and climbs, with the stream down on your right. The creek valley expands, allowing the intermittent stream to do some weaving as it makes its way.

At 2.8 miles, the trail moves away from the creek and continues climbing at a pretty good pitch.

As you approach mile 3, a sign indicates the trail makes a sharp switchback and climbs some steps. A lesser trail goes to the right. At the next switchback, a sign indicates a Civilian Conservation Corps (CCC) quarry to the left. Walk out to this area for a little exploring and a chance to rest from the constant uphill. You'll see markings in the rock, evidence of explosive rods used to break rock for construction.

Back on the main trail, you're still climbing now on the wide tread of the old roadbed used by the CCC to transport rock uphill for construction of the park buildings. At 3.3 miles, veer left and follow CR 268. The trailhead parking comes into view as you turn. It's possible to cross the road here, but there's no need to if you're heading back to the trailhead. It's a nice easy walk to the trailhead, completing this 3.5-mile hike.

Once you forget how much the last climb hurt, you'll realize what a wonderful hike this was. The Indian Rockhouse alone is worth the admission price of the climb out.

Nearby Attractions

Wild Bill's Outfitter rents canoes, kayaks, rafts, and johnboats and offers lodging (870-449-6235; wildbillsoutfitter.com).

Tyler Bend Visitor Center has exhibits, informational brochures, and a beautiful deck out back. Tyler Bend also includes a campground without hookups. The gravel beach area at Tyler Bend is a popular and busy place during the warmer months (870-439-2502; nps.gov/buff).

Directions

From Yellville, drive south on AR 14. Turn left onto County Road 268 and drive 6 miles. Drive past a right turnoff to camping and river access. Watch for cabins on your right and then trailhead parking on the right.

Buffalo National River:
Rush Ghost Town

SCENERY: ★ ★ ★ ★ ★
TRAIL CONDITION: ★ ★ ★ ★
CHILDREN: ★ ★ ★ ★
DIFFICULTY: ★ ★ ★
SOLITUDE: ★ ★ ★

AN OLD STOREFRONT STILL STANDS AT RUSH.

GPS TRAILHEAD COORDINATES: N36° 07.895' W92° 34.091'

DISTANCE AND CONFIGURATION: 4.6-mile out-and-back

HIKING TIME: 3 hours

HIGHLIGHTS: Historical structures, zinc mines, historical mining relics, and views of Rush Creek

ELEVATION: 525' at trailhead, 682' at highest point

ACCESS: Open 24/7; no fees or permits required

MAPS: USGS *Rea Valley;* Trails Illustrated *Buffalo River East Half*

FACILITIES: None

WHEELCHAIR ACCESS: No

COMMENTS: No pets allowed on this trail. The 0.3-mile Morning Star Interpretive Loop passes several historical structures and is an alternative short hike.

CONTACTS: Buffalo National River, Buffalo Point Ranger Station, 870-449-4311, nps.gov/buff

Overview

Rush is an Arkansas ghost town. It was a mining community that began in the 1880s and thrived through the 1920s because of its rich deposits of zinc. Zinc was used to protect metal from corrosion and in the manufacture of copper and brass. Rush was most active during World War I, when demand for zinc peaked.

Rush began to decline along with the declining demand for zinc and was finally abandoned in the late 1960s. Neil Compton, who led the effort to designate the Buffalo River as a national river, had intimate knowledge of the river. In his book, *The Battle for the Buffalo River,* he wrote, "There had been another flurry of mining activity during and after the Second World War, but by 1969 Rush was bereft of inhabitants except for Gus Setzer and Fred Dirst, an old miner who conducted tours into the mines for wandering visitors. . . ." You won't get any tours into the zinc mines today, but you can walk through history on a trail leading past old structures, equipment, and many abandoned mines.

Route Details

As you're facing the trailhead kiosk, begin walking to the left (west), following a trail that parallels the road. This is a wide gravel tread. Interpretive signs line the trail at points of interest. The story of Rush can be found on the Buffalo National River website.

You'll come quickly to an ore smelter. It is the oldest structure in Rush, dating to 1886. Holders of the Morning Star mining claim sought to discover silver but were disappointed. As it turned out, zinc was discovered in January of 1887.

At 0.1 mile, look to your left (southwest) and you'll see the hub of the community of Rush just across Rush Creek where you drove into the ghost town. You're looking down on the Taylor–Medley Store and home. It remained in operation until the 1950s.

You'll come quickly to the blacksmith shop that operated from 1925 to 1931. After the blacksmith shop at 0.2 mile, you pass an

Buffalo National River: Rush Ghost Town

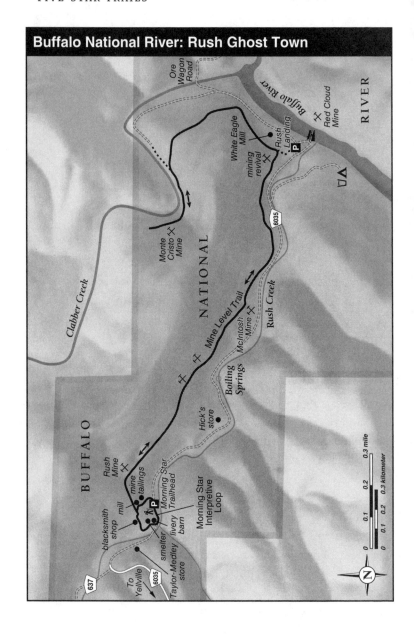

intersection on your right that takes you back to the Morning Star Trailhead where you began, forming a short loop hike. You might opt to take this short section on the return trip of this out-and-back.

Continue straight (east) and uphill to the abandoned zinc mine level. At 0.3 mile, a spur trail to the left takes you a short distance to a closed-off mine. You'll continue to pass many mine entrances similar to this as you walk this trail and could easily spend an entire day exploring every historical site along the route.

Off to your right, you might get some nice views into the town of Rush. It would be interesting to get into a time machine and see what this area was like during the 1920s.

At 0.6 mile, an ore cart sits next to the trail. Its heavy iron construction has stood the test of time and the elements. At 0.7 mile, cross some tailings from a mine. You may spot Rush Creek down below and the mountains across the valley to the southeast.

When floating conditions are good, you'll hear lots of traffic as floaters drive to Rush Landing, a popular Buffalo River access point on the other end of town, where Rush Creek feeds into the river.

At 0.9 mile, you'll descend steeply, and then the trail turns left, leaving the roadbed you've been hiking. A sign indicates this turn. It would be easy to continue downhill here and miss the trail. For a kid-friendly version of this hike, you might consider turning around here

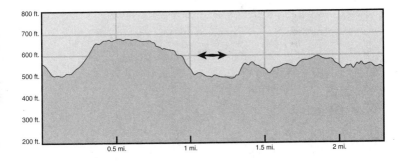

for a 2-mile out-and-back. You could then spend more time exploring the little loop trail close to the trailhead.

The trail continues to do some ups and downs along the base of a small bluff area. At 1.1 miles, you come to a little bluff outcrop for a nice view. At 1.3 miles, it's easy to go off trail by accident. Watch for the trail to turn left and head uphill through a bluff area. This is a well-built trail, but narrower now and skirting some tall drop-offs. At 1.5 miles, you'll pass a sinkhole on your left and piles of mining tailings.

Just past 1.5 miles, come to an intersection. Turning left takes you up above Clabber Creek. Turning right takes you to the Clabber Creek Trailhead. Continue left to Clabber Creek. This trail doesn't take you down to creek level, but water may be available at springs along the bluffs. At 1.8 miles, you may get a glimpse of an old tin-roofed narrow building downhill on the right.

At just over 2 miles, take a left on Ore Wagon Road and begin climbing. At the end of the climb, you'll come to some large mechanical items next to the trail. At 2.3 miles, come to the end of the maintained trail and the edge of the Buffalo National River boundary. Turn around here and hike back to where you began to complete this 4.6-mile hike.

Be sure to explore Rush Creek after your hike. The water is cold and clear. It's a great place to splash around and cool off.

Nearby Attractions

Buffalo Point Ranger Station is small but carries books and gifts related to the area. An RV campground with hookups is available on one of the beautiful bluff-lined portions of the Buffalo River (870-449-4311; nps.gov/buff).

Directions

From Yellville, take AR 14 East and drive 11.5 miles. Watch for the RUSH sign and turn left onto Marion County Road 6035, a paved road. Drive 4 miles into the historical ghost town of Rush. The trailhead and kiosk will be on your left after the low-water bridge over Rush Creek.

20 # Blanchard Springs and Mirror Lake Trail

SCENERY: ★ ★ ★ ★ ★
TRAIL CONDITION: ★ ★ ★ ★ ★
CHILDREN: ★ ★ ★ ★
DIFFICULTY: ★ ★
SOLITUDE: ★ ★

BLANCHARD SPRINGS FLOW YEAR-ROUND FROM THE BASE OF THIS BLUFF.

GPS TRAILHEAD COORDINATES: N35° 57.546' W92° 10.544'

DISTANCE AND CONFIGURATION: 1.7-mile loop

HIKING TIME: 1 hour

HIGHLIGHTS: Blanchard Springs, Mirror Lake, and historical remains of John Blanchard's 1880s mill

ELEVATION: 410' at trailhead, 416' at highest point, 347' at lowest point

ACCESS: Open 24/7; no fees or permits required

MAPS: USGS *Fifty-Six*

FACILITIES: Restrooms, camping, and picnic area

WHEELCHAIR ACCESS: There is access to the spring and a fishing area on Mirror Lake. The trail around Mirror Lake is not accessible.

COMMENTS: Leashed pets are allowed. Fishing is available on Mirror Lake with an Arkansas fishing license. Hike early in the morning and you might have the spring to yourself.

CONTACTS: Blanchard Springs Caverns, 870-757-2211, blanchardsprings.org

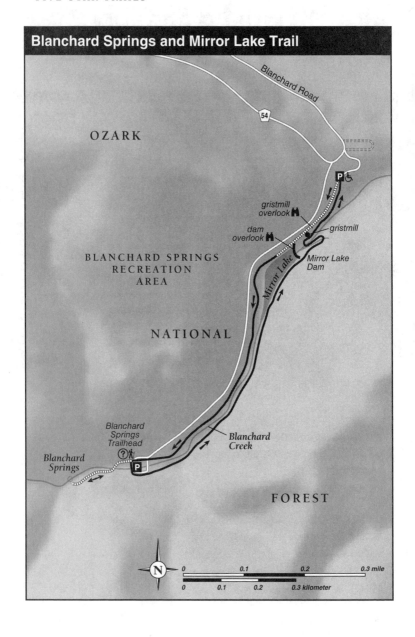

Blanchard Springs and Mirror Lake Trail

OZARK

Blanchard Road

54

gristmill overlook

dam overlook

gristmill

BLANCHARD SPRINGS
RECREATION
AREA

Mirror Lake

Mirror Lake Dam

NATIONAL

Blanchard
Springs
Trailhead

Blanchard
Creek

Blanchard
Springs

FOREST

N

| 0 | 0.1 | 0.2 | 0.3 mile |
| 0 | 0.1 | 0.2 | 0.3 kilometer |

Overview

Blanchard Springs and Mirror Lake Trail is one of the shorter hikes in this book, but a lot of beauty is packed into 1.7 miles. The spring invites visitors to wade in the water, and you'll almost always find a crowd. Mirror Lake lives up to its name, reflecting the beauty of its surroundings, and Blanchard's Mill is a fascinating place to explore.

Route Details

Begin with a short walk to Blanchard Springs, the water source for Mirror Lake. From the trailhead kiosk, walk 0.1 mile to the Blanchard Springs overlook. The S-shaped bridge across Blanchard Creek is a work of art. You'll quickly arrive at the spring that flows year-round. Steps lead down to the water, but use caution because rocks in the creek are slick.

Return to the trailhead parking area and then walk to the right (south then east) along the side of a massive bluff around a circle drive. Shortly, you'll come to an opening in the rock wall next to an arched stone bridge. The trail takes you downstream to the right of the creek. During the wet season, several small drainages will be flowing across this trail into the creek.

You'll enjoy beautiful views down to the creek and then across Mirror Lake. After you pass the dam down to your left, the gristmill

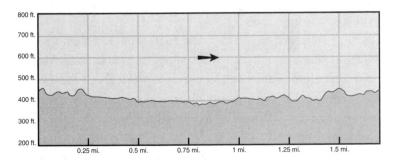

comes into view below the dam. Watch for a turn at 0.8 mile that swings to the left and takes you down to a wet crossing in front of the gristmill. This left turn is easy to miss because a lesser trail continues down the creek.

Just before you cross the creek, watch for the rock shelter that's carved into the south side of the creek below the dam. If the water level is low, you can explore this area before crossing.

You'll want to explore the gristmill. John Blanchard built this undershot gristmill in the 1880s. It sits downstream from Mirror Lake Dam, testifying to the hardworking people who once made their lives in the Ozarks. The Civilian Conservation Corps restored the dam and part of the mill during the 1940s. The waterwheel is long gone, but much of the stone structure remains.

After you cross the creek, the trail comes to a junction. To the left is a short spur to the base of the dam. Turn right, walking downstream along the left side of the creek. At 1.0 mile, the trail turns left and goes up to a wheelchair-accessible parking area and boardwalk. Follow the boardwalk south with the sounds of the creek below and the road above on the right.

At almost 1.1 miles, you'll come to the mill overlook and then the dam overlook. At the dam and just before beginning to walk on the fishing dock, there are steps up to the road and a parking area, but you'll continue on the trail. Walk along the fishing dock, enjoying views across Mirror Lake.

After leaving the fishing dock, walk with Blanchard Creek upstream and on your left. There is some splitting of the trail through this section, but continue upstream and past a blue hole in the creek. Step carefully and stay centered in the trail because you're walking above a short bluff. Slipping from the trail here could result in a tumble down to the creek.

At 1.5 miles, the trail switchbacks down to creek level. At 1.6 miles, you'll come to some steps that take you up to the road. Take a left on the road and walk back to the trailhead to complete this hike.

GRISTMILL BUILT BY JOHN BLANCHARD IN THE 1880s AND RESTORED BY THE CCC IN THE 1940s

I like to take a second look at the springs and add another couple of tenths of a mile to the hike.

Nearby Attractions

Ozark Folk Center State Park displays and preserves the crafts and music of the Ozarks region. Well-known professional and amateur musicians often perform in the large auditorium (ozarkfolkcenter. com). Cabins are available in the park, and an RV campground is located next door; for more information, call 800-264-3655.

Directions

From Mountain View, follow AR 14 West 5.4 miles, then turn left (west) and continue on AR 14 toward the town of Fifty-Six. Drive 6.5 miles and arrive at the Blanchard Springs Caverns entrance 1.0 mile before Fifty-Six. Turn right into Blanchard Springs. Drive 1.5 miles and pass the Blanchard Springs Caverns entrance and visitor center. After 1.0 more mile, turn right and drive past Mirror Lake on your left to the circle drive at the entrance to Blanchard Springs.

Petit Jean State Park:
Seven Hollows Trail

SCENERY: ★ ★ ★ ★ ★
TRAIL CONDITION: ★ ★ ★ ★
CHILDREN: ★ ★ ★
DIFFICULTY: ★ ★ ★ ★
SOLITUDE: ★ ★ ★

THIS NATURAL BRIDGE STANDS ABOVE THE TRAIL.

GPS TRAILHEAD COORDINATES: N35° 06.855' W92° 56.724'

DISTANCE AND CONFIGURATION: 4.5-mile loop

HIKING TIME: 3 hours

HIGHLIGHTS: Natural bridge, grotto, turtle rocks, and small caves

ELEVATION: 897' at trailhead, 906' at highest point

ACCESS: Open daily, sunrise–sunset; no fees or permits required

MAPS: USGS *Adona;* available at visitor center and lodge

FACILITIES: None

WHEELCHAIR ACCESS: No

COMMENTS: Leashed pets are allowed.

CONTACTS: Petit Jean State Park, 501-727-5441, petitjeanstatepark.com

Overview

Hike through a diversity of environments and geological features on this hike. You'll visit lush and thick forest floors within four of the area's seven hollows. You'll cross ridges between the hollows that feature turtle rocks and nearly desert environments with great variation in plant and animal habitats. You'll also see a natural bridge and a grotto.

Route Details

The Seven Hollows Trail is marked with blue diamond vinyl markers. There are mile markers every 0.5 mile, but their accuracy is questionable.

The trail begins with a short, level stretch through a young pine grove. This area was burned in 2000 by a widespread fire that put the lodge and other parts of the park at risk. You'll see some evidence of the fire, but the forest has recovered to a great extent. The most notable evidence is the young age of the pines along the beginning of the trail and on the ridges between the hollows.

After about 400 feet, you'll arrive at an intersection to the loop. Turn left and follow the loop clockwise. The first section of this route is exposed to the sun due to the burn, so watch for wildflowers. Begin a gradual descent into the first hollow. You'll walk through some sandy patches that seem to slow you down a little, but this doesn't last long.

At 0.4 mile, come alongside a small stream that formed this first hollow and crisscross it several times. The hollows contain a variety of towering hardwoods, while the trail passes through scrubby adolescent pines. The fire of 2000 scorched the ridges but left the hollows virtually untouched.

At 0.5 mile, come into a nice bluff area, suitable for exploration. The trail veers left and crosses the creek before climbing slightly with the stream down on your right. At 0.7 mile, cross the creek again, putting the stream down on your left. Just after crossing the creek,

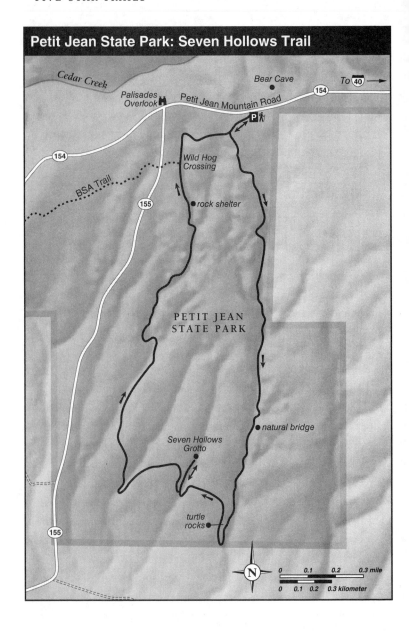

Petit Jean State Park: Seven Hollows Trail

Cedar Creek

Bear Cave

To 40

Palisades
Overlook

Petit Jean Mountain Road

154

P

154

Wild Hog
Crossing

BSA Trail

155

● rock shelter

PETIT JEAN
STATE PARK

● natural bridge

Seven Hollows
Grotto
●

turtle
rocks ●

155

N

| 0 | 0.1 | 0.2 | 0.3 mile |

| 0 | 0.1 | 0.2 | 0.3 kilometer |

you'll see a small shelter cave up on your right. These little caves are fun for kids to explore.

Just past the cave, cross the stream again, placing you on the left side of the stream and bringing you past several small caves and some larger overhanging bluffs.

Begin a climb at 0.8 mile. This is a nice place to pause and look back over your right shoulder at the bluffs you just passed. You'll gradually move a little farther away from the creek. Watch for expansive views of the bluffs over on the other side of the hollow. You might notice the stream picking up volume as you go.

At 1.2 miles, arrive at the natural bridge. This is a beautiful little area to explore. You can walk under the bridge for better views of its shape and then return underneath the bridge back to the trail.

Cross the creek at 1.5 miles. If you need water, this might be a good spot for filtering. You'll cross the creek a couple more times, with great spots for a little foot soaking along the way.

At 1.6 miles, come alongside a short bluff on your left. Enjoy a nice walk under the overhang, sporting lots of plants in this rich environment.

At almost 1.7 miles, turn right and climb on top of the bluff, entering a totally different environment. You'll see examples of "turtle rocks" formed by erosion. You might even spot the rare collared lizard scurrying across the rocks.

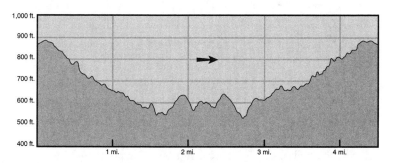

After 1.8 miles, take a left and head back into the woods through a small pine and hardwood area. After mile 2.0, begin to descend into another hollow. You might notice steps carved into rocks on this trail. This trail work was done by the Civilian Conservation Corps in the 1930s.

Watch for a sign pointing to the grotto. Turn right and follow a rocky trail to a nice, enclosed, small canyon with a pool of water. During the wet season, a small waterfall flows at the far end of the grotto. This is a great place for lunch and a break. If you sit quietly in this area, especially early in the morning, you might spot some wildlife.

Follow the spur trail back to the main trail and turn right, continuing on the main trail. You've now covered 2.3 miles. Climb to a second rocky ridge and pass through more turtle rock. You can easily get a case of déjà vu when you cross the turtle rocks. At 2.4 miles, the trail turns back into the woods on your left. Watch for this because it's easy to continue along this open ridge and miss the trail.

At 2.6 miles, begin descending, and hike through some split rocky sections that are a treat to pass through. You'll descend into this larger hollow, crossing the creek bed, and begin climbing at a good clip with the creek bed down on your right. You'll come up on a new ridge pretty quickly at 2.8 miles and continue down the trail with the hollow down to your right.

Continue following the trail at roughly the same elevation for a while; eventually you'll see deeper woods down to your left as you skirt another hollow. At close to 3.2 miles, you'll walk across a wide bridge rock. Begin descending slightly with a short bluff on your right. The trail turns left and descends, passing mile marker 3, but you did the grotto, and that added some distance to your mileage.

At 3.3 miles, cross the stream that formed this hollow, meandering along with some nice views in these open woods. At 3.5 miles, the hollow deepens and bluff heights increase. You'll come to a division in the hollow where a bluff point becomes pronounced in the center. At 3.6 miles, come alongside an overhanging bluff with lots of little caves. If you like big rocks and huge blufflines, pause to take in this section. Listen for a variety of birds.

At 3.8 miles, you'll feel enveloped in bluffs as they rise all around. At 3.9 miles, a short spur trail crosses the creek to a neat rock shelter.

At 4.0 miles, you'll notice the BSA (Boy Scouts of America) Trail turning off to the left. Continue straight, following the blue diamonds. You'll begin coming out of the last hollow before coming to the original trail you entered on earlier. When you reach the intersection at 4.4 miles, turn left and walk the short distance back to the trailhead, completing the trail with 4.5 miles.

Nearby Attractions

The Museum of Automobiles was established in 1964 by Winthrop Rockefeller (501-727-5427; museumofautos.com). For a reasonable admission price, visitors will view some beautiful automobiles. Petit Jean State Park is well known for its annual antique car show.

Mount Magazine State Park has a restaurant, lodge, cabins, hiking trails, and a campground with RV hookups (479-963-8502; mountmagazinestatepark.com).

Mount Nebo State Park has cabins and hiking trails with walk-in campsites (479-229-3655; arkansasstateparks.com/mountnebo).

Directions

To get to Petit Jean State Park from I-40, take Exit 108 for AR 9 South toward Morrilton. After 7.5 miles, turn right onto AR 154 West and drive 11 miles to Petit Jean State Park.

Mather Lodge is 1.5 miles past the visitor center. After you pass the turnoff to the lodge, continue on AR 154 0.8 mile farther west or a total of 2.3 miles from the visitor center. You'll pass Bear Cave Trail on the right and immediately come to Seven Hollows Trail on the left (south) side of the road.

Petit Jean State Park:
Cedar Falls Trail

SCENERY: ★ ★ ★ ★ ★
TRAIL CONDITION: ★ ★ ★ ★
CHILDREN: ★ ★ ★ ★
DIFFICULTY: ★ ★ ★
SOLITUDE: ★ ★

CEDAR FALLS

GPS TRAILHEAD COORDINATES: N35° 07.005' W92° 56.334'

DISTANCE AND CONFIGURATION: 2-mile out-and-back

HIKING TIME: 1.5 hours

HIGHLIGHTS: Cedar Falls and Cedar Creek

ELEVATION: 888' at trailhead, 888' at highest point, 592' at lowest point

ACCESS: Open 24/7; no fees or permits required

MAPS: USGS *Adona;* available at lodge and visitor center

FACILITIES: Restroom, restaurant, rooms, cabins, and campgrounds are available at Mather Lodge and the park visitor center.

WHEELCHAIR ACCESS: No

COMMENTS: Leashed pets are allowed.

CONTACTS: Petit Jean State Park, 501-727-5441, petitjeanstatepark.com

Overview

See Cedar Falls, one of Arkansas's best-known waterfalls, estimated to be 95 feet tall. Hike along beautiful Cedar Creek en route to the falls on this nationally recognized trail located in Arkansas's first state park, established in 1923.

Route Details

The trailhead begins behind Petit Jean State Park's Mather Lodge. Pause to admire the Civilian Conservation Corps (CCC) construction evident in parts of the lodge. Spend a few minutes at the breezeway taking in the views of the valley behind the lodge. You'll be hiking down into that valley momentarily.

It's easy to see why the land around Cedar Falls was the first land designated by the State of Arkansas for the purpose of building a state park. During the years of 1933–38, the CCC built many of the structures still in use today at Petit Jean State Park.

From the overlook, the trail begins to your left at a kiosk a short distance away. This is a short but demanding hike due to the climb back out on the return trip.

Just after the trailhead, you'll come to an intersection. Turn right and continue downhill on the Cedar Falls Trail, following 2-by-6-inch orange painted blazes. Turning left would take you on a connecting trail to Bear Cave Trail, but you have Cedar Falls in your sights for this hike.

Cedar Falls Trail is heavily used, so please stay on the marked path. You'll see evidence of damage from shortcuts up and down the series of switchbacks during the first portion of this hike. This is a well-constructed trail, so stay on the path and enjoy every step.

You'll be hiking down with a small stream to your left. When there's water, you'll see and hear some beautiful cascades along this section.

At just after 0.2 mile, the trail levels out, still following the stream toward Cedar Creek. At 0.4 mile, cross Cedar Creek over a

Petit Jean State Park: Cedar Falls Trail

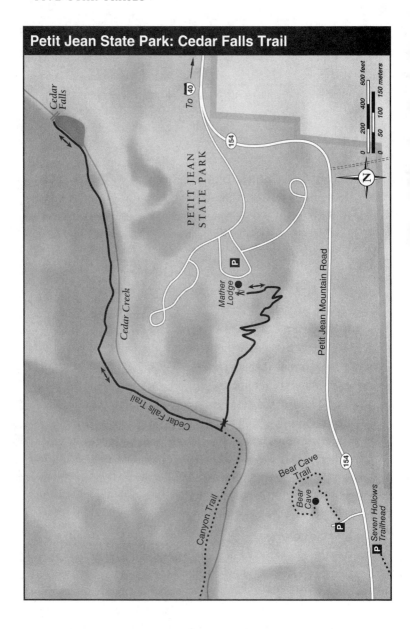

nice bridge. Turn right after crossing and hike northeast up Cedar Creek. You'll pass house-size boulders along the way and many beautiful pools in Cedar Creek.

At exactly 1.0 mile, you'll arrive at Cedar Falls. If the water is flowing, you've been hearing it for a while during your approach. There are many vantage points from which to enjoy these falls, and lots of boulders to crawl over and sit on as you take in the falls.

Return to the trailhead by the same route you came to complete this 2-mile hike. Enjoy your climb up and out. Take your time and enjoy the views.

Nearby Attractions

The Museum of Automobiles was established in 1964 by Winthrop Rockefeller (501-727-5427; museumofautos.com). For a reasonable admission price, visitors will view some beautiful automobiles. Petit Jean State Park is well known for its annual antique car show.

Mount Magazine State Park has a restaurant, lodge, cabins, hiking trails, and a campground with RV hookups (479-963-8502; mountmagazinestatepark.com).

Mount Nebo State Park has cabins and hiking trails with walk-in campsites (479-229-3655; arkansasstateparks.com/mountnebo).

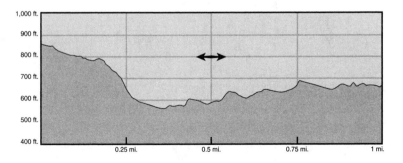

Directions

To get to Petit Jean State Park from I-40, take Exit 108 for AR 9 South toward Morrilton. After 7.5 miles, turn right onto AR 154 West and drive 11.0 miles to Petit Jean State Park and past the visitor center on your right. Drive 1.5 miles past the visitor center to Mather Lodge. The Cedar Falls Trailhead is at the overlook behind the lodge breezeway.

Mount Magazine State Park: Ridge and High Point Loops

SCENERY: ★ ★ ★ ★ ★
TRAIL CONDITION: ★ ★ ★ ★
CHILDREN: ★ ★ ★
(*Signal Hill Trail:* ★ ★ ★ ★ ★)
DIFFICULTY: ★ ★ ★
SOLITUDE: ★ ★ ★

VIEW FROM THE EDGE OF MOUNT MAGAZINE

GPS TRAILHEAD COORDINATES: N35° 10.459' W93° 37.186'

DISTANCE AND CONFIGURATION: 5.7-mile figure eight

HIKING TIME: 3.5 hours

HIGHLIGHTS: Expansive ridgeline vistas and a visit to the highest elevation in Arkansas

ELEVATION: 2,445' at trailhead, 2,753' at highest point

ACCESS: Open 24/7; no fees or permits required

MAPS: USGS *Blue Mountain;* available at visitor center

FACILITIES: Restrooms and camping available at the visitor center. Cabins, rooms, and a restaurant are available at the Mount Magazine Lodge.

WHEELCHAIR ACCESS: No

COMMENTS: Leashed pets are allowed.

CONTACTS: Mount Magazine State Park, 479-963-8502, mountmagazinestatepark.com

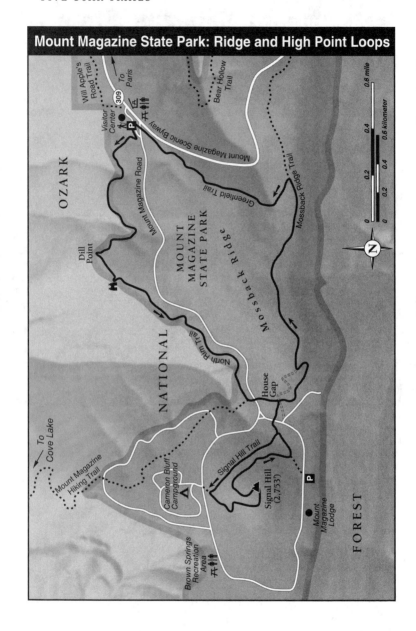

Mount Magazine State Park: Ridge and High Point Loops

Overview

Mount Magazine boasts the highest elevation in Arkansas with temperatures as much as 10–15°F cooler than surrounding areas. Mount Magazine State Park is home to Arkansas's Butterfly Festival each June, and the mountain is known for the variety of butterfly species it attracts. This hike combines the North Rim, Mossback Ridge, Signal Hill, and Greenfield Trails to form a figure eight hike, capitalizing on scenic vistas and crossing the wooded high point of Arkansas.

Route Details

Begin your hike on the North Rim Trail at the Mount Magazine Visitor Center. The trailhead is on the west end of the parking area. The trail is marked with orange blazes (round metal trail markers). The path begins slightly downhill on a wide tread and soon features nice views to your right into the valley. At 0.2 mile, you'll cross School Creek.

All along this westward-leading trail, you'll enjoy expansive views to the north. Watch for wind-blown, dwarfed oak trees along the ridge. At 0.6 mile, you'll cross Dill Creek. At almost 0.8 mile, the canopy opens up, and you come to Dill Point, a nice rock outcrop with great views to the north. Continuing on the main trail, you'll pass occasional outcrops where you can take in the views. During fall and winter, when trees lose their leaves, you'll have views all along this section.

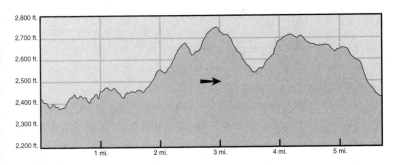

At 1.4 miles, you may walk through a seeping spring next to the trail. Up this high, the watershed is limited, so most creek crossings will be dry or a mere trickle unless there have been recent rains.

Arrive at an intersection at 1.8 miles and veer left to access the Mossback Ridge Trail. Cross Mount Magazine Road on Mossback Ridge Trail, marked with round yellow markers. Turning right would take you down the North Rim Trail to the north side of the Cameron Bluff Campground, but for this hike, don't go that way.

At 2.0 miles, turn right (northwest) toward Signal Hill Trail and the highest point in Arkansas. Cross Lodge Road and then come to a junction with the Signal Hill Trail. Turn right to hike Signal Hill Trail counterclockwise and begin walking uphill through mixed hardwoods on this heavily used route. As you walk through these woods nearing the top of Mount Magazine, there are no open vistas, but the woods are beautiful. A brochure that corresponds to occasional interpretive marker numbers is available at the visitor center.

At 2.5 miles turn left (southwest). Turning right would take you to Cameron Bluff Campground. Continue on the loop another 0.4 mile and arrive at the highest point in Arkansas 3.0 miles into the hike. You'll find a survey marker and a map of Arkansas formed from rocks. You may sign the registration book located in a mailbox and take a break on log benches. From the high point, follow the main trail left of the large wooden high-point sign and begin a downhill walk toward Mount Magazine Lodge.

Turn left (east) at 3.3 miles and head back toward the Mossback Ridge Trail. Going straight here would add a short out-and-back to Mount Magazine Lodge. The Skycrest Restaurant inside the lodge is a great stop for a meal or a break.

Continuing toward Mossback Ridge, you'll pass a concrete slab that used to be the foundation for a water pump. You'll arrive at the intersection where you began Signal Hill Trail. Turn right (east) and cross Lodge Road at 3.5 miles, then take another right turn onto Mossback Ridge Trail marked with yellow blazes. Shortly, you'll pass a junction with a roadbed to the left, but stay right, following yellow blazes. Mossback follows the ridge, going slightly uphill and to the east. This wide ridge makes for some easy walking.

At 4.6 miles, come to a junction with the Greenfield Trail. A sign points left to the visitor center. Turn left (northwest) onto the Greenfield Trail, now approximately a mile from the visitor center. This trail is marked with green blazes. At 4.8 miles, you'll cross Big Shoal Creek, an intermittent stream that flows down into Bear Hollow, eventually carving out a beautiful valley farther to the east.

AR 309 comes into view at about 5.2 miles, and you'll descend a gravel section of trail and arrive at the road at 5.5 miles. Turn left to follow the road northeast without crossing, and watch for the visitor center a short distance down the road. Arrive back at the North Rim Trailhead at 5.7 miles. Be sure to stop in at the visitor center to check out the history and geology displays, as well as the butterfly garden.

Nearby Attractions

Mount Magazine State Park has a restaurant, lodge, cabins, hiking trails, and a campground with RV hookups (479-963-8502; mount magazinestatepark.com).

Mount Nebo State Park has cabins and hiking trails with walk-in campsites (479-229-3655; arkansasstateparks.com/mountnebo).

Petit Jean State Park has a restaurant, lodge, cabins, hiking trails, and a campground with RV hookups (501-727-5441; petitjean statepark.com).

Directions

This loop trail begins at the Mount Magazine Visitor Center, located across from the Greenfield Picnic Area at the junction of AR 309 (Mount Magazine Scenic Byway) and the road to Cameron Bluff Overlook. From Paris, drive south on AR 309 (South Elm Street/Mount Magazine Scenic Byway) toward East Pine Street 1.0 mile. Turn left onto AR 309 and drive 16.4 miles, arriving at the Mount Magazine Visitor Center on your right.

Missouri Ozarks

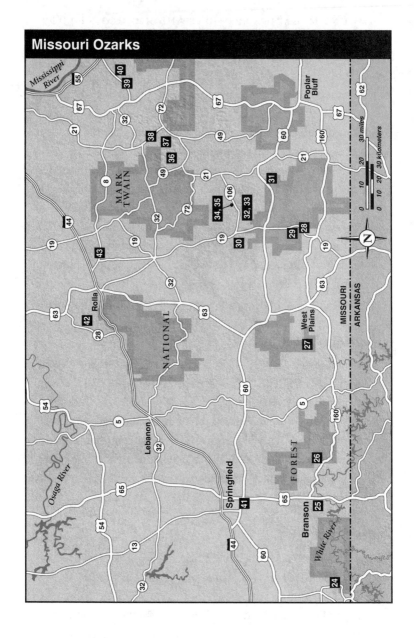

Missouri

24 Roaring River State Park:
Fire Tower, Deer Leap, Devil's Kitchen, and River Trails

ROARING RIVER SPRING

GPS TRAILHEAD COORDINATES: N36° 34.778' W93° 49.839'

DISTANCE AND CONFIGURATION: 5.6-mile figure eight with out-and-back spur

HIKING TIME: 3.5 hours

HIGHLIGHTS: Roaring River Spring, Roaring River, Devil's Kitchen, and Devil's Spring

ELEVATION: 1,056' at trailhead, 1,418' at highest point

ACCESS: Open 24/7; no fees or permits required

MAPS: USGS *Eagle Rock*

FACILITIES: Restrooms, visitor center, nature center, restaurant, lodge, picnic areas, and camping

WHEELCHAIR ACCESS: No

COMMENTS: Leashed pets are allowed.

CONTACTS: Roaring River State Park, 417-847-2539, mostateparks.com/park
/roaring-river-state-park

Overview

This hike combines parts of the Fire Tower, Deer Leap, Devil's Kitchen, and River Trails. These are great stand-alone trails, but they combine to give us a nice length and a chance to see a variety of features. You'll see Roaring Spring, the state's 10th largest spring with a daily output of 22 million gallons. You'll see some large trout in the holding pool that extends from the spring and lots of unique rock formations in the Devil's Kitchen area.

Route Details

This hike begins at the Ozark Chinquapin Nature Center, connecting several trails to form two loops, taking us through some of the most scenic parts of Roaring River State Park. Look for the Fire Tower Trail around the right side of the nature center. Step inside for a trail guide that includes points of interest for the Devil's Kitchen Trail that you'll be hiking later.

Follow the trail to the right of the building and up to County Road F. Turn right (east) and follow the road a short distance. Cross CR F when you see the trailhead at about 0.1 mile from the nature center. Watch for traffic as you cross this often-busy paved road. The Fire Tower Trail is marked with brown vinyl blazes.

After entering the woods, immediately turn right and walk the trail with the road down to your right. Shortly, you'll veer left and begin a steep climb past a small BEAR AWARE sign. After about 50 yards, turn left and continue up, following an old roadbed. When this climb tops out, you'll be walking along a broad bench for a short distance before climbing some more. The woods through this section are open, with a healthy canopy of beautiful mixed hardwoods. At 0.6 mile, you'll finally top out and begin walking in the woods, enjoying views on both sides of this ridge.

At 1.0 mile, you'll pass the intersection with a connector trail marked with white blazes that leads to the Deer Leap Trail. You'll use this trail when you return to this spot after visiting the fire tower.

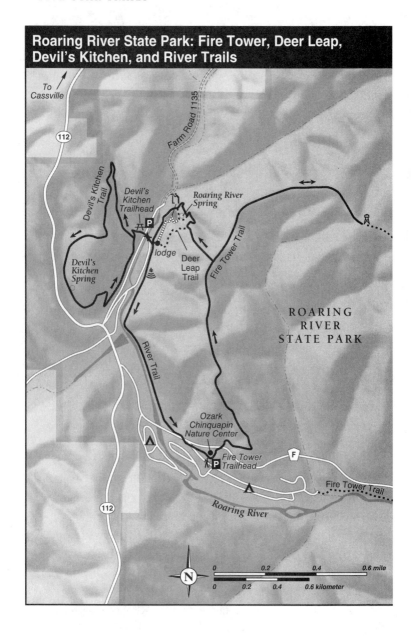

Roaring River State Park: Fire Tower, Deer Leap, Devil's Kitchen, and River Trails

To Cassville

112

Farm Road 1135

Devil's Kitchen Trail

Devil's Kitchen Trailhead

Roaring River Spring

Fire Tower Trail

lodge

Devil's Kitchen Spring

Deer Leap Trail

ROARING RIVER STATE PARK

River Trail

Ozark Chinquapin Nature Center

Fire Tower Trailhead

F

Fire Tower Trail

112

Roaring River

N

0		0.2		0.4		0.6 mile
0	0.2	0.4		0.6 kilometer		

Stay to the right on the Fire Tower Trail and enjoy some smooth sailing through this level section. There are lots of wildflowers during the spring and summer seasons along this high ridge.

At 1.8 miles, you'll arrive at the fire tower built by the Civilian Conservation Corps (CCC) during the 1930s. It's open, and you may climb up to see what it feels like to be in the upper parts of the tree canopy. The trail is adjacent to the Roaring River Cove Hardwood Natural Area, containing some hardwoods that have not been logged for many years. It's a nice place to hang out.

After checking out the fire tower, backtrack on the Fire Tower Trail to the Deer Leap Trail connector trail junction you passed earlier. At 2.5 miles, come to the connector trail, marked with white blazes. Turn right (northwest) and follow Deer Leap Trail downhill. At 2.7 miles, the trail turns right, giving you a good view of the fish hatchery when leaves are off the trees. Continue down several switchbacks. You'll descend many limestone steps carefully placed by the CCC. Pause to admire their work. This is a heavily used section of the trail, and shortcuts by hikers have caused damage to the hillside. Please stay on the trail.

At 2.8 miles, make a sharp right onto Deer Leap Trail, marked with green vinyl blazes. Turning left takes you to a small spring and a boardwalk down to the Hatchery Overlook, well worth doing if you

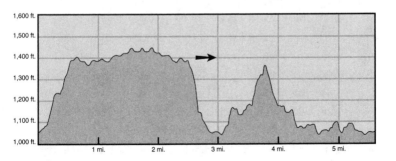

have time for a short out-and-back. But for your larger loop hike, turn right at 2.8 miles and follow the trail downhill and down stairs to Roaring River Spring at the base of a huge dolomite bluff. The interpretive sign next to the spring says divers have measured the spring's vent to a depth of 215 feet. Roaring River Spring lost some of its "roar" in 1880 when the dam was built to retain the spring's water, but cascading water downstream gives you a hint of the sound. Notice the size of some of the trout in the holding pool above the dam and next to the spring. Rare flooding of the area makes for some trophy trout fishing downriver.

After exploring Roaring River Spring, continue along the sidewalk past the large hatchery pool on your left and rearing pools to your right. At 3.1 miles, you'll come to the CCC lodge. Turn right, crossing Roaring River on a small bridge, and watch for traffic.

Look for the Devil's Kitchen Trailhead across the road at 3.2 miles. This loop trail is 1.5 miles long, and you'll enjoy every step. As you walk into the woods, you'll follow a small hollow. At just after 3.2 miles, turn right and step uphill alongside a bench, hiking Devil's Kitchen Trail counterclockwise to follow the park's interpretive brochure. Walk along this bench with sounds of the river down to your right and a small bluff lining the trail on your left.

At 3.5 miles, you'll come to the confluence of a couple of small streams that may have water. At 3.9 miles, the trail turns and moves away from the sounds of the river as the trail levels out.

At 4.1 miles, you'll pass Devil's Kitchen Spring up to the left of the trail. You'll feel cold air coming from the opening in the bluff and enjoy some beautiful clear water. Treating this water before drinking is recommended. At 4.3 miles, you'll find the Devil's Kitchen area on the left side of the trail. This is a good area for exploration, with tumbling rocks everywhere.

Shortly after Devil's Kitchen, an intersection to the right takes you to Hatchery Road, but you should continue left and follow the trail back to the trailhead. At 4.6 miles, you'll arrive at the spur you hiked earlier, leading back to Devil's Kitchen Trailhead.

After leaving Devil's Kitchen Trail, cross Roaring River as you did earlier and head over to the CCC lodge. Turn right and go into the woods on the River Trail, following yellow blazes. An alternative is to walk along the river downstream, but if you do, you might need to dodge flying bait in this popular trout fishing location.

The River Trail passes an amphitheater and then comes alongside an overhanging bluff with a pool in the river to the right. This is a nice place for a break in the shade of this bluff with the cool river pool below.

At 5.4 miles, come out of the woods and walk next to the campground across the road on your right. Cross CR F with caution, and the Ozark Chinquapin Nature Center comes into view. Arrive back at the nature center to complete your hike at 5.6 miles.

Directions

From Cassville, take MO 112 South 6.2 miles. Turn left onto CR F and drive 0.6 mile, then veer right to the Ozark Chinquapin Nature Center.

Ruth and Paul Henning Conservation Area:

Homesteaders Trail

THE VIEW ACROSS COX'S BALD GLADE

GPS TRAILHEAD COORDINATES: N36° 41.017' W93° 17.283'

DISTANCE AND CONFIGURATION: 3.7-mile loop

HIKING TIME: 2.5 hours

HIGHLIGHTS: Historical water wells, rock walls, and glade areas

ELEVATION: 825' at trailhead, 1,098' at highest point

ACCESS: Open 24/7; no fees or permits required

MAPS: USGS *Garber*

FACILITIES: None

WHEELCHAIR ACCESS: No

COMMENTS: Leashed pets are allowed.

CONTACTS: Missouri Department of Conservation, Southwest Regional Office, 417-895-6880, tinyurl.com/henningca

Overview

How is it that you could be hiking through deep woods after a 15-minute drive from downtown Branson, Missouri? The speed of driving through development on MO 65 gives way to a peaceful walking pace on the Homesteaders Trail alongside a beautiful creek and 14-foot waterfall. You'll see evidence of early inhabitants of the area, such as abandoned water wells, rock walls, ponds, and glades used by early homesteaders.

Ruth and Paul Henning provided this land that is now a conservation area on the northwest edge of Branson. Mr. Henning was a writer and producer, responsible for several TV classics such as *Beverly Hillbillies, Green Acres,* and *Petticoat Junction.* Mr. Henning died in 2005 but would be pleased to know that his gift is being enjoyed and protected.

Route Details

Homesteaders Trailhead parking is on the south side of Sycamore Church Road just before the Roark Creek low-water bridge. Begin by walking across the low-water bridge to the kiosk then up several steps. You quickly come to a junction and turn left. You're walking with Roark Creek flowing downstream on your left, hiking the loop clockwise. You'll see nice rock formations along this section, a small tributary to Roark Creek, and a rocky path with short blufflines up on your right.

The trail is marked with square hiker insignias. Trail markers are color coded; Homesteaders Trail is orange. At just over 0.1 mile, you come off the bench and back down toward the creek level. Watch for large sycamore trees, which love growing alongside creeks.

Come to an intersection where a lesser trail comes in from the right, but the main trail is marked straight. At 0.3 mile, a service road comes in from the left that says DO NOT ENTER. The trail is clearly marked, and you veer right to begin following an old roadbed uphill

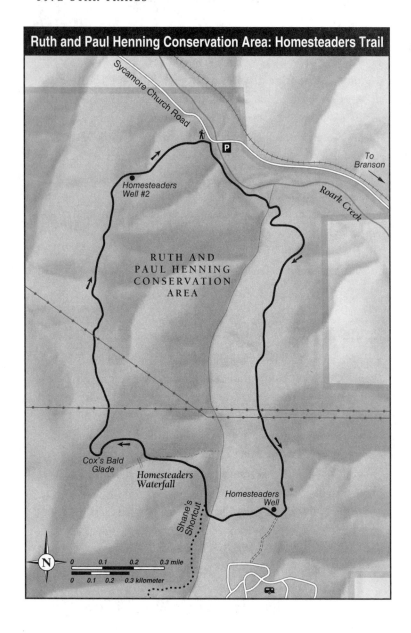

Ruth and Paul Henning Conservation Area: Homesteaders Trail

Sycamore Church Road

P

To Branson

Roark Creek

Homesteaders Well #2

RUTH AND PAUL HENNING CONSERVATION AREA

Cox's Bald Glade

Homesteaders Waterfall

Shane's Shortcut

Homesteaders Well

N

0   0.1   0.2   0.3 mile
0   0.1   0.2   0.3 kilometer

at a pretty good clip. This is a good place to shed a layer of clothes if you're hiking in cooler weather.

Homesteaders Trail is a great early-morning hike for solitude since this is close to Branson. It's also a good time to see deer and other wildlife. The old roadbed continues to wind and climb. At 1.1 miles, walk under a power line, and you might see an airport tower in the distance before walking back into the woods.

A small pond is located a short distance off the trail on the left at about 1.4 miles. Hiker-dog thought it was fine, but I would double filter it before drinking. It was a little murky.

At 1.5 miles, you'll arrive at a junction where the trail turns right, leaving the old roadbed. After following this clearly marked right turn, you immediately come to an old homesteader's well. It is deep and covered with a grill. I was extra careful while taking photos so that my camera didn't become a historical artifact at the bottom of the well.

Shortly after the well, the trail descends to a creek bed. At 1.7 miles, the trail crosses a larger streambed. In wet seasons, this will be a wet crossing. After crossing, you'll see Shane's Shortcut coming in from the left. Our route on the Homesteaders Trail continues straight ahead with the creek down on your right.

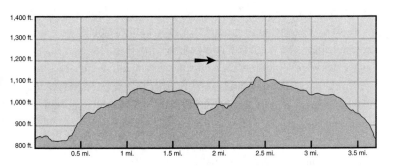

HOMESTEADERS WELL

Just after mile 2, the trail splits for a short distance, with the left route being the safer of the two. The trail comes to a 12- to 14-foot waterfall and a nice view down the creek. Stay well away from the upstream side of the waterfall because slick rock leads to the edge. On the other side of the waterfall, begin an immediate climb out of the drainage.

You'll climb through Cox's Bald Glade at 2.3 miles. Glades are sometimes called balds, and they were significant in local history. Post–Civil War vigilante groups used the balds as meeting places so they could see if anyone was approaching the area. As a result, vigilantes were sometimes called baldknobbers. Enjoy the view, then continue into the forest and cross another power line clearing. At 2.7 miles, pass evidence of homesteaders as the trail trends downward and then passes under another smaller power line.

At 3.3 miles, come to another water well and then an impressive rock wall that crosses a small drainage. At this point, I realized that I didn't want this hike to end. I found myself wanting to turn around and head back the other way around the loop. The last portion of the trail is a steep downhill, so watch your step because your legs may be a little tired from the hike.

You'll see a fence to the left of the trail and houses on the other side. Go down two sets of crosstie steps before coming back to the trailhead to complete this 3.7-mile hike.

Nearby Attractions

Sycamore Log Church is a great stop for photos. It's still a functioning church, and a brochure at the entrance tells its history and schedule of services (417-230-4789; sycamorelogchurch.org).

The City of Branson is known for its tourist attractions. Be prepared for traffic jams if you visit during the warmer months (Chamber of Commerce: 417-334-4084; bransonchamber.com).

Table Rock State Park has hiking trails, a large campground with RV hookups, and very nice showers (417-334-4704; mostateparks.com/park/table-rock-state-park).

Directions

From MO 65, north of Branson, turn west onto MO 465 South 2.3 miles. Take the MO 248 ramp to Branson/Reeds Spring, then turn left onto MO 248 East and drive 0.4 mile. Turn right onto Sycamore Church Road (County Road 248-20) and drive 3.5 miles to the Ruth and Paul Henning Conservation Area parking area just before the low-water bridge across Roark Creek. The trailhead is across the low-water bridge.

26

Hercules Glades
Wilderness: West Loop

SCENERY: ★ ★ ★ ★
TRAIL CONDITION: ★ ★ ★ ★
CHILDREN: ★ ★ ★
DIFFICULTY: ★ ★ ★
SOLITUDE: ★ ★ ★

LONG CREEK FALLS

GPS TRAILHEAD COORDINATES: N36° 41.112' W92° 57.576'

DISTANCE AND CONFIGURATION: 6.5-mile loop

HIKING TIME: 4 hours

HIGHLIGHTS: Expansive views from open limestone glades to deep forests and cedar ridges; Long Creek Falls and Devil's Den on Long Creek

ELEVATION: 1,066' at trailhead, 1,340' at highest point

ACCESS: Open 24/7; no fees or permits required

MAPS: USGS *Hilda*

FACILITIES: Primitive campsites, picnic tables, and a pit toilet at the trailhead

WHEELCHAIR ACCESS: No

COMMENTS: Leashed pets are allowed. Drinking water is not available at the trailhead. You may filter from Long Creek. There are no blazes on the trail, so carry a map and compass.

CONTACTS: Hercules Glade Wilderness, Mark Twain National Forest, 573-364-4621, tinyurl.com/herculesglade

Overview

Hercules Glades Wilderness is named for the historical town of Hercules, established in 1891. Hercules was located on MO 125 at what is now the eastern border of Missouri's second-largest wilderness area. Legend has it that an early traveler was astonished at the rugged landscape and named the town after the Greek god.

On this hike, you'll see that rugged landscape up close and experience some of the beauty that makes Hercules Glades Wilderness a top location recommended by anyone who has hiked in Missouri. High, open forests contrast with dry, grassy rock glades punctuated with cedar groves and the beauty of Long Creek, which flows through the wilderness area.

Route Details

Begin this hike at the Coy Bald Trailhead, entering at the kiosk. Walk about 500 feet and come to the wilderness boundary. Immediately after the boundary, you'll see the returning trail from this loop hike coming in on your left, but continue straight.

You'll find yourself walking through the first of many cedar groves mixed with some oaks and other hardwoods on what used to be the continuation of Cross Timber Road. This trail is high and dry, so you'll want to carry enough water to get you to Long Creek, the first chance to refill.

At about the first mile, you'll descend into some deeper woods. You finally get into some hilly hiking, ending with a steep climb that comes out at 1.7 miles on a beautiful glade with some open views across a valley toward the north.

This overlook is an easy place to wander off the trail. The trail turns to the right (south), moving uphill on the glade. Then watch for the trail to reenter the woods on your left pretty quickly. If you get to a fire ring, you've probably followed a short spur and need to back up a little and look for where the trail reenters the woods.

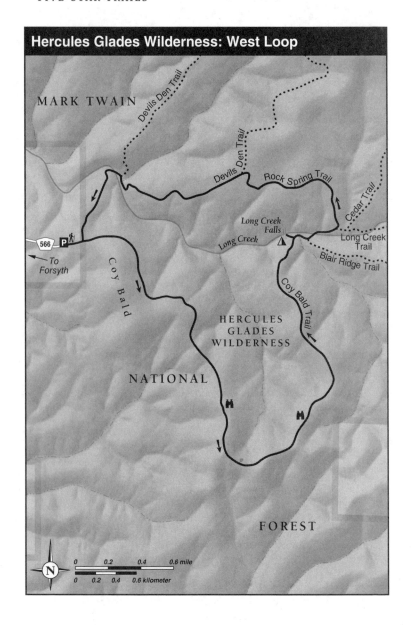

Hercules Glades Wilderness: West Loop

MARK TWAIN

Devils Den Trail

Devils Den Trail

Devils Den Trail

Rock Spring Trail

Cedar Trail

Long Creek Falls

566

P

To Forsyth

Long Creek

Coy Bald

Long Creek Trail

Blair Ridge Trail

HERCULES GLADES WILDERNESS

Coy Bald Trail

NATIONAL

FOREST

N

| 0 | 0.2 | 0.4 | 0.6 mile |
| 0 | 0.2 | 0.4 | 0.6 kilometer |

You'll come to a small pond on the left side of the trail at 2.1 miles. This water could be filtered, but you'd probably want to prefilter with a bandanna to avoid clogging your water filter. Hiker-dog likes her water with a little grit, so this pond was just the thing to revive her.

The trail continues on the level before climbing slightly and passing some large white oak trees overlooked by loggers years ago. You may notice large hardwoods with wide limbs intermingled with cedar trees that grew up around them as the thicker forest infringed on the area.

At 2.7 miles, you'll come to an open glade to the left with expansive views. This is a great place for springtime wildflowers. Continue walking along this glade ridge, and then meander through cedar groves with a different character than the hardwoods from earlier in the hike.

At 3.1 miles, begin descending back into hardwoods tangled with cedars, then into deeper woods. As you get to the lower section of this area, you arrive at a field of oddly shaped boulders alongside the trail.

At 3.8 miles, you arrive at a junction to the left and right. The left spur leads to a campsite close to the beautiful Long Creek Falls. Going straight is the main trail, but it's worth taking that short spur to the left to see the waterfall before returning to this junction. There

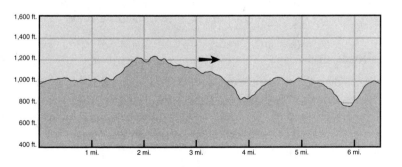

are no blazes, so keep your eyes peeled for the route. Be sure to carry a map and trail notes on this hike.

The main trail goes upstream along the right (south) side of the creek, crossing a small drainage. The trail becomes pretty evident and climbs to a junction where you'll see a campsite and a junction to Blair Ridge Trail on the right. Bear left and follow the trail downhill, crossing Long Creek at 3.9 miles and continuing on the other side, still going upstream.

At 4.1 miles, you'll come to a junction with a lesser trail and veer left. Continue up and top out on the climb after 0.5 mile before enjoying some easy walking in the woods. Just keep your eyes open for the trail tread. At 5.2 miles, you'll cross a lesser trail, but continue straight on the main, and sometimes eroded, trail through a cedar grove as you trend downhill, making your way back to Long Creek.

At 5.8 miles, come to Devils Den on Long Creek. The trail crosses the creek and then climbs a short distance to a campsite on your right. Continue climbing until you come to the original trail you began on earlier. Turn right and return to the trailhead to complete this 6.5-mile hike.

Nearby Attractions

Branson, a popular vacation destination, is located 45 minutes to the east of Coy Bald Trailhead. For more information, visit the Branson Area Chamber of Commerce (417-334-4084; bransonchamber.com).

Directions

From Forsyth, drive 9 miles east on MO 160 and turn left onto Forest Road 566 (Cross Timbers Road). Drive approximately 4 miles, arriving at the Coy Bald Trailhead. There is parking available at this location.

Devils Backbone
Wilderness: Blue Spring Loop

BLUFFS ON THE NORTH FORK WHITE RIVER IN THE MORNING SUN

GPS TRAILHEAD COORDINATES: N36° 45.380' W92° 09.216'

DISTANCE AND CONFIGURATION: 10-mile balloon

HIKING TIME: 7 hours

HIGHLIGHTS: Blue Spring ("Little Blue Spring"), Crooked Branch, and an example of a devil's backbone ridge

ELEVATION: 717' at trailhead, 1,138' at highest point

ACCESS: Open 24/7; no fees or permits required

MAPS: USGS *Cureall NW, Dora,* and *Siloam Springs*

FACILITIES: Restrooms, camping, and picnic areas; water available during the warmer seasons

WHEELCHAIR ACCESS: No

COMMENTS: An optional 4-mile out-and-back from Blue Spring to the edge of North Fork White River is perfect for a few hours and a picnic. Hunting and fishing are allowed with the appropriate licenses.

CONTACTS: Devils Backbone Wilderness, Mark Twain National Forest, 573-364-4621, tinyurl.com/devilsbackbonewa

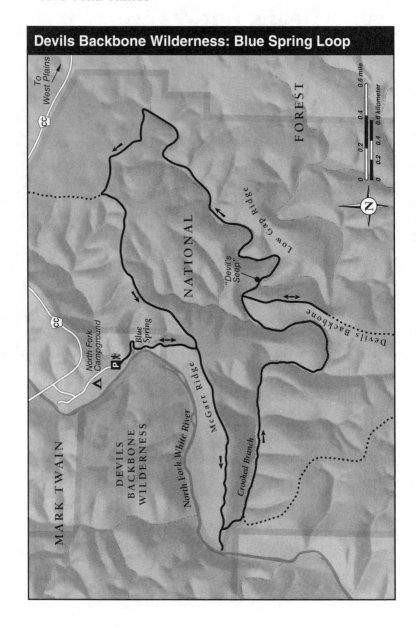

Devils Backbone Wilderness: Blue Spring Loop

Overview

On this hike, you'll visit Blue Spring, climb along some blufflines, then take a pleasant walk down to a perfect place for a picnic next to the North Fork of the White River. Then, get deep into the Devils Backbone Wilderness, eventually climbing onto an example of a backbone, a high narrow ridge with views through the trees to the east and west.

I should probably call this Little Blue Spring on North Fork White River, so it isn't confused with the Blue Spring on the Current River described in another hike. This is a much smaller spring at 7 million gallons per day. It sits next to the river and is a special place to visit.

There are no blazes on this lengthy hike, and trail conditions can vary depending on the season. If you're not comfortable with route-finding or the length of this hike, the 4-mile out-and-back to the edge of North Fork White River is an excellent alternative.

Route Details

Begin at the Blue Spring Trailhead on the south end of the North Fork Campground. Take the trail that leads to the left and crosses a small bridge over an intermittent stream, arriving at Blue Spring at 0.2 mile. You may see vinyl white trail blazes on the first section to Blue Spring. After the spring, you will probably not see any more blazes or signs on this trail.

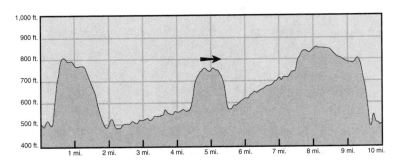

"LITTLE" BLUE SPRING NEXT TO THE NORTH FORK WHITE RIVER

After passing the spring, climb at a pretty good clip and take in views of the North Fork White River down on your right. You'll see an occasional large, scraggly oak, which left me wondering if these were overlooked during logging years ago.

When you reach a junction at 0.6 mile, turn right (west). You'll see this junction again much later in the hike if you do the whole loop. Begin walking along McGarr Ridge, an easy stroll trending slightly down, with the North Fork White River on your right.

The rate of descent increases and you might see some eroded sections. As you descend, you'll pass a trail coming in from the left at 1.9

miles. You'll return to this junction to continue the loop hike, but visit the river first. Continue straight to the North Fork White River and take a break. There are gravel bars suitable for wading if water levels are low. You'll see several social trails from those who've camped here.

After enjoying the view and possibly filtering some water for the next section of the trail, where water may not be available, backtrack to the intersection you passed a few minutes before and turn right (south) to begin following Crooked Branch. At just over 0.1 mile, you may notice a trail junction leading to the right, but continue straight following Crooked Branch. You'll follow this streambed for a while.

At 4.4 miles, begin watching to your right for a route leading up to Devils Backbone. This out-and-back spur is 0.6 mile for a 1.2-mile round-trip, but it's worth the climb. There are views through the trees to the west and east. You're looking across the Crooked Branch drainage that wraps almost all the way around this ridge. After walking across the narrow "backbone," the ridge begins to widen slightly, so turn around and return to the loop trail.

After coming back down from the "backbone," turn right and walk about 0.1 mile where Crooked Branch goes to the right (south), and you'll continue straight (southeast) into Mary Hollow. You might notice some stone pavers on the trail where you cross Crooked Branch drainage.

On my first hike of this area, I was low on water, and all of the creeks were dry. My black Lab buddy, Hiker-dog, found water at the base of the bluff on the left side of the trail along this section. I was so excited to find water that I added a waypoint for "Devil's Seep," my name for the spot. If you're hiking the whole loop in drier times of the year, be sure to carry plenty of water.

You'll be in Mary Hollow for a while. It will narrow from time to time, and you'll zigzag across the streambed several times. It's easy walking in Mary Hollow, but keep your eyes peeled to stay on the trail, and watch for patches of greenbriers in this low area. You'll pass through some spots with massive tangled vines suitable for swinging.

One vine suspended over the middle of the trail tempted me to grab hold and glide for a few yards.

At just under 2.5 miles from the top of the saddle of the Devils Backbone, or 7.5 miles into the total hike, you'll notice a hollow that comes in from the right. Don't go that way, but continue straight, watching for the trail. This would be an easy spot to wander up into the wrong hollow.

Watch for a trail to your left leading uphill at 7.7 miles. Depending on the season, this could be easy to miss, as I did on my first time through.

At 8.3 miles into the total hike distance, you'll arrive at a junction with a trail leading to McGarr Trailhead on MO CC 0.5 mile away. Don't go that way. Turn left and follow an old roadbed generally southwest for 1.2 miles back to the Blue Spring spur junction. Enjoy some high and level walking here. You may notice a lesser path on your left 0.2 mile past the McGarr Trailhead junction. Don't take that route, which heads down to McGarr Hollow.

At 9.4 miles, come to the junction and turn right, backtracking to Blue Spring. Be sure to stop and admire the spring one more time before completing this 10-mile hike.

Directions

From West Plains, take MO CC West 16 miles to North Fork Campground and Recreation Area on your left. Drive through the campground to the southeast and park in the circle drive at the Blue Spring Trailhead.

28

Mark Twain National Forest: Greer Spring Trail

SCENERY: ★ ★ ★ ★ ★
TRAIL CONDITION: ★ ★ ★ ★ ★
CHILDREN: ★ ★ ★ ★
DIFFICULTY: ★ ★ ★
SOLITUDE: ★ ★ ★

ONE OF TWO GREER SPRING OUTLETS

GPS TRAILHEAD COORDINATES: N36° 46.786' W91° 20.760'

DISTANCE AND CONFIGURATION: 2-mile out-and-back

HIKING TIME: 1.5 hours

HIGHLIGHTS: A large, scenic hollow leads to Greer Spring with two large outlets, one from a cave and the other from the bottom of the Greer Spring Branch.

ELEVATION: 878' at trailhead, 878' at highest point, 600' at lowest point

ACCESS: Open 24/7; no fees or permits required

MAPS: USGS *Greer*

FACILITIES: Pit toilets at the trailhead

WHEELCHAIR ACCESS: No

COMMENTS: Leashed pets are allowed. Coming back up and out of Greer Spring is a good climb. This is a great hike for kids, but all need to step carefully around slick rocks close to the spring channel.

CONTACTS: Mark Twain National Forest, Eleven Point Ranger District, 573-996-2153, tinyurl.com/greerspring

Mark Twain National Forest: Greer Spring Trail

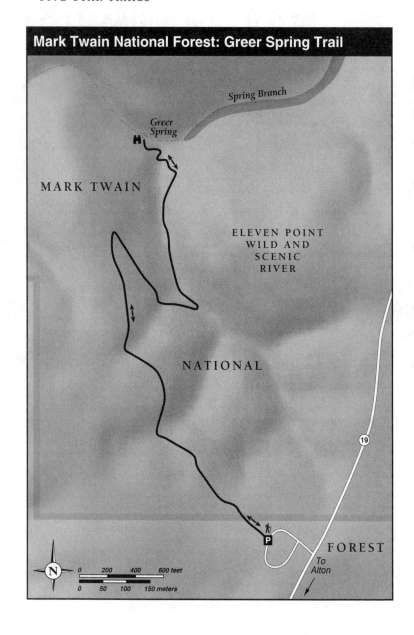

Spring Branch

Greer Spring

MARK TWAIN

ELEVEN POINT
WILD AND
SCENIC
RIVER

NATIONAL

FOREST

To
Alton

19

N

0	200	400	600 feet
0	50	100	150 meters

Overview

This is a short hike that packs a powerful visual punch. You'll see the second-largest spring in Missouri and a beautiful rocky valley. Greer Spring is named for Samuel Greer, who built Greer Mill downstream on Greer Branch. The mill site is on private property, but the spring is what you're here to see.

Route Details

The trailhead is on the west side of scenic MO 19. You'll be immediately impressed with this well-built trail that switchbacks down toward Greer Spring. You'll pass several wooden benches and nicely built little bridges. Greer Spring Trail could be described as 1 mile in and 3 miles back out, but the distance is the same both ways. You might take advantage of those benches on the hike up and out.

After a couple of sweeping switchbacks, the trail arrives at Greer Spring Overlook at 1 mile. Metal stairs lead down to the water level. One spring outlet is from a cave upstream on your left. Another outlet is just downstream in the middle of the branch channel to your right. A path from the overlook going downstream allows you to view the lower outlet. This whole area is beautiful in sights and sounds. Bring your camera and stay awhile. After enjoying Greer Spring, backtrack to the trailhead to complete this 2-mile hike.

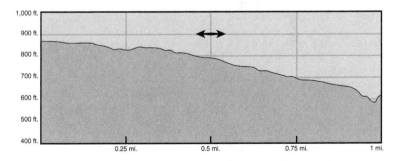

Nearby Attractions

Greer Recreation Area on the Eleven Point River is 1 mile north of Greer Spring on MO 19. It offers camping, picnic tables, restrooms, and a boat ramp.

Turner Mill is worth the dirt-road drive if you have time for exploring. Turner Mill North Picnic Area is accessed by gravel Forest Road 3152. The turnoff to Turner Mill is 15 miles south of Winona or 11 miles north of Alton on MO 19. From MO 19, turn onto Forest Road 3152 for 6 miles, then onto FR 3190 for 3 miles.

Directions

Greer Spring Trailhead is on the west side of MO 19 about 8 miles north of Alton, Missouri, or about 1 mile south of the MO 19 bridge over Eleven Point River.

29

Ozark Trail: McCormack Lake to Greer Crossing Campground

ELEVEN POINT RIVER

GPS TRAILHEAD COORDINATES: N36° 049.364' W91° 21.044'

DISTANCE AND CONFIGURATION: 8-mile balloon

HIKING TIME: 5 hours

HIGHLIGHTS: Expansive views of Eleven Point River and Boom Hole Vista and a beautiful walk close to the edge of Eleven Point River

ELEVATION: 598' at trailhead, 945' at highest point

ACCESS: Open 24/7; no fees or permits required

MAPS: USGS *Greer*

FACILITIES: A primitive campground is on the west side of McCormack Lake. Pit toilets and picnic tables are on the east day-use side of the lake where the trailhead is located.

WHEELCHAIR ACCESS: No

COMMENTS: An optional shorter hike could be to Boom Hole Vista as an out-and-back of 3 miles.

CONTACTS: Ozark Trail Association, 573-436-0540, ozarktrail.com

SCENERY: ★ ★ ★ ★ ★
TRAIL CONDITION: ★ ★ ★
CHILDREN: ★ ★
(★ ★ ★ ★ *from McCormack Lake to Boom Hole as an out-and-back*)
DIFFICULTY: ★ ★ ★
SOLITUDE: ★ ★ ★

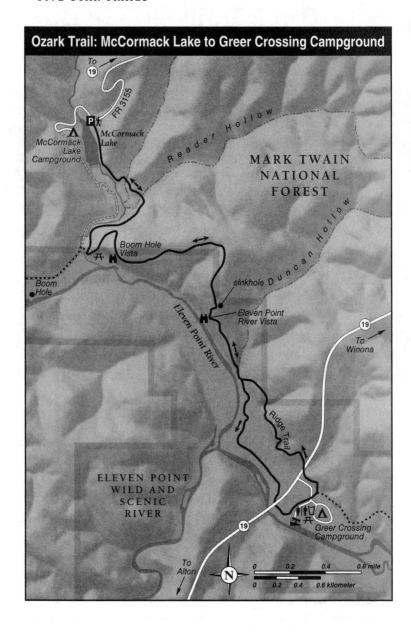

Ozark Trail: McCormack Lake to Greer Crossing Campground

To 19

FR 3155

P

McCormack Lake Campground

McCormack Lake

Reader Hollow

MARK TWAIN NATIONAL FOREST

Duncan Hollow

Boom Hole Vista

Boom Hole

sinkhole

Eleven Point River Vista

Eleven Point River

19

To Winona

Ridge Trail

ELEVEN POINT WILD AND SCENIC RIVER

19

Greer Crossing Campground

To Alton

N

0   0.2   0.4   0.6 mile

0   0.2   0.4   0.6 kilometer

Overview

You'll visit a beautiful vista over Eleven Point River on this Ozark Trail out-and-back hike. You'll also see Eleven Point River up close and have a chance to get wet if you like. The Ozark Trail (OT) owes its existence to the efforts of many volunteers who build and maintain the trail. Watch for the iconic white blazes with an interlocking *OT* that mark the Ozark Trail.

Route Details

Begin this hike on the day-use side (east) of McCormack Lake. Looking at the lake from the parking lot, you'll see that the trail begins to the left and follows south alongside the lake. At the spillway, the path takes a left and climbs up to a junction at 0.3 mile. Stay to the right, heading southeast. Shortly, pass through some nice hardwoods and cross an old roadbed at 0.5 mile.

Just after the roadbed, come down to a couple of washes in Reader Hollow. As you climb the sides of the hollow, you may see a small stream that flowed out of the McCormack Lake spillway winding its way toward Eleven Point River.

At 1.1 miles, arrive at a junction with the Ozark Trail (OT) and take a left, walking to the northeast. You're now following the OT along the north side of the Eleven Point River. Begin a beautiful

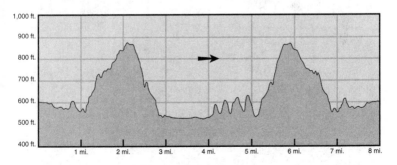

climb up to a bluff, arriving at Boom Hole Vista at 1.5 miles. You'll find a picnic table and split rail cedar post fence. This is a great stop for pictures and a lunch break. It's also a good turnaround spot if you don't want to do the longer hike.

During a period of heavy logging between 1890 and 1910, virgin pine logs cut from the surrounding hilltops were placed on a chute and sent off the top of the bluff. The logs hit the river with a loud boom, hence the name Boom Hole. The logs floated downstream to Decker Shoal. From there, the logs were hauled to Winona on log trains.

HIGH BLUFF VIEW OF THE ELEVEN POINT RIVER

Continuing past the Boom Hole Vista on the high bench, there are several other outcrops with views down to Eleven Point River. The trail eventually veers away from the bluffs into open woods.

At 2.5 miles, the trail turns right and joins a roadbed for a few yards before arriving at a small sinkhole on the left. The trail then descends a rocky crag, crossing a small rocky glade. The glade forms natural steps that carry you down the trail to a river view at 2.5 miles. During winter, notice how the sycamore trees stand out against the background with their light-colored bark along the sides of the river below. In the fall, enjoy broad views of color across the river.

The trail begins to follow along a cedar-pine mixed forest, very different in character than the hardwoods at the higher elevations. At 3.0 miles, the trail turns left, away from the river, and follows Duncan Hollow a short distance. Continue on the OT back to the river's edge, coming to a junction on the left with the Ridge Trail at 3.1 miles. This is where you'll return from Greer Crossing Campground later in the hike. Continue straight on the OT and notice the sandy soil under your feet. You'll pass a nice spot to walk out to the river's edge at 3.3 miles. This is a great place to get your feet wet.

At 3.8 miles, the MO 19 bridge comes into view to your right. The trail veers right and goes down under the bridge. This spot is confusing because you'll see OT blazes straight toward the Greer Recreation entrance *and* to the right toward the bridge. If you accidentally go straight or miss the junction, it's not a problem. Just hike to the road and down toward the campground, where you'll intersect with the trail coming from under the bridge.

Notice how much stronger the Eleven Point River flow has become. This is due to Greer Spring, which fed into the river from the west side upstream. Greer Spring is said to be the second-largest spring in Missouri and once powered Greer Mill (named after Samuel Greer). This beautiful spring is featured in the hike on page 173.

Cross under the bridge at 3.7 miles. The rocky tread winds downstream after the bridge and then comes into the Greer Recreation

Area parking lot. You'll come to the picnic area and past a water station and restrooms that will be open during warmer months.

At about 4.1 miles, pass the entrance to the campground, and then come to a junction sign indicating the OT to the right and McCormack Lake to the left. Turn left and head back on the Ridge Trail, climbing steeply into a cedar grove. Pretty quickly, you'll come down and cross MO 19. You can see the entrance to Greer Recreation Area to your left. After crossing the highway, the trail climbs on the ridge and gives you a good workout. There are a couple of tough little climbs, then things level out on the ridge.

You'll come back down to the junction with the OT that you hiked earlier at 5.4 miles. This should look familiar. Turn right on the OT, back toward McCormack Lake. You'll enjoy backtracking the remaining miles, especially seeing views of Eleven Point River in different light of the day. Arrive at McCormack Lake to complete this 8-mile hike.

Nearby Attractions

Greer Spring Trail is located on the west side of MO 19, about 8 miles north of Alton, Missouri, or about 1 mile south of the MO 19 bridge over the Eleven Point River. See the trail description on page 173 to add this short and scenic hike to your itinerary.

Directions

The turnoff to McCormack Lake Recreation Area is 13 miles south of Winona on MO 19. From Winona, go south on MO 19 13 miles, then go west on Forest Road 3155. The lake is about 2 miles down this road, which is drivable in any vehicle.

Ozark National Scenic Riverways:
Alley Spring and Mill

ALLEY MILL

GPS TRAILHEAD COORDINATES: N37° 09.106' W91° 26.525'

DISTANCE AND CONFIGURATION: 2-mile balloon

HIKING TIME: 1.5 hours

HIGHLIGHTS: Alley Spring and Mill, Alley Branch, intricate bluffs, and small caves

ELEVATION: 651' at trailhead, 847' at highest point

ACCESS: Open daily, sunrise–sunset; no fees or permits required

MAPS: USGS *Alley Spring*

FACILITIES: Restrooms, picnic area, covered pavilion, and Alley Spring Museum

WHEELCHAIR ACCESS: Access is available from the parking lot to the mill, but not on the Overlook Trail or Alley Branch Trail.

COMMENTS: Leashed pets are allowed.

CONTACTS: Ozark National Scenic Riverways, 573-323-4236, nps.gov/ozar

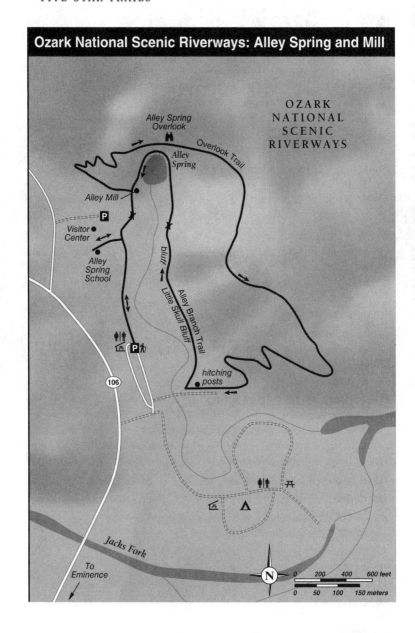

Ozark National Scenic Riverways: Alley Spring and Mill

OZARK
NATIONAL
SCENIC
RIVERWAYS

Alley Spring
Overlook

Overlook Trail

Alley
Spring

Alley Mill

P

Visitor
Center

Alley
Spring
School

bluff

Alley Branch Trail
Little Skull Bluff

P

106

hitching
posts

Jacks Fork

To
Eminence

N

| 0 | 200 | 400 | 600 feet |
| 0 | 50 | 100 | 150 meters |

Overview

This little trail packs a lot of scenery into 2 miles. You'll be immersed in beauty every step of the way. Alley Spring, managed by the National Park Service, is a deep blue and flows across beautiful rocky cascades into Alley Branch. Alley Mill is a fantastic structure and well worth a look inside if it's open when you visit. In addition to the paved routes around the schoolhouse and mill, you'll get a dose of trail hiking on the Overlook and Alley Branch Trails.

Route Details

The trail begins at the kiosk on the northeast side of the parking area. Follow the sidewalk north 0.1 mile, then take a short spur to a one-room schoolhouse on your left. Return to the main path, turning left then right to cross a bridge leading to Alley Mill. The paved path leads to the left (west) side of the mill, coming quickly to an intersection. Turn left and take the unpaved Overlook Trail. The trail switchbacks up the hill. Admire this beautifully designed trail.

The trail tops out, and you'll hear the sounds of the spring below, quite impressive given the distance from the water. You might hear the one-room schoolhouse bell too. At about 0.5 mile, you'll arrive at a stone overlook with an interpretive sign and a view back down to the mill and Alley Branch.

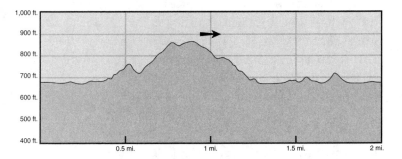

GATES CONTROL WATER FLOW TO THE TURBINE MILL.

Continue climbing gradually along the upper ridge of the Alley Spring valley. You're walking along a ridge with slight drop-offs on both sides. Watch for large hardwoods that you couldn't begin to wrap your arms around.

The trail descends switchbacks lined with a black igneous rock then arrives at an intersection with a dirt road at 1.2 miles. This dirt road serves as a horse trail. Turn right (west) and follow the dirt road a short distance, passing between two hitching posts. You'll see a bridge up ahead, but it leads back to the parking lot. Turn right just after the hitching posts and follow the Alley Branch Trail upstream with the stream down on your left. Eighty-one million gallons of water flow from Alley Spring daily, making it the sixth- or seventh-largest spring in Missouri, depending on who's counting.

The trail passes what I call Little Skull Bluff at 1.4 miles. Be careful along this stream because there isn't much of a shore, and the bottom of the creek drops off quickly. You're likely to see evidence of beavers in the area.

At 1.5 miles, you'll come to stone steps and a second bluff area before coming back down to a junction with a beautiful view of the mill. There's a bridge to your left, but continue straight, climbing another set of steps. You'll pass a beautiful cascade as you come up to Alley Spring at 1.6 miles. This is a great place to explore and take some photos. The trail circles partway around the spring and arrives at the mill on the turbine side at about 1.7 miles.

After passing the mill, return to the parking lot the way you came to complete this 2-mile hike. If you have time, and it is open, check out the inside of this three-floor mill. Alley Mill used a Leffel Turbine horizontal mill that allowed operators to control the mill speed, making it preferred to the older overshot or undershot vertical wheels.

Nearby Attractions

Alley Spring Campground, with tent and RV facilities, is on the west side of MO 106. From Alley Spring and Mill, drive 0.4 mile south on MO 106 and turn right into the campground (573-323-4236).

Ruby's Family Restaurant is a great place to meet local folks and learn about the area. Ruby's serves up good, home-cooked food with friendly service (573-226-3878).

Directions

From the intersection of MO 19 and MO 106 in Eminence, Missouri, drive west on MO 106 5.7 miles to the entrance of Alley Spring on the right. The trailhead and information kiosk are located next to the sidewalk on the east side of the parking area.

Ozark National Scenic Riverways:
Big Spring Double Loop

SCENERY: ★ ★ ★ ★ ★
TRAIL CONDITION: ★ ★ ★ ★ ★
CHILDREN: ★ ★ ★ ★
DIFFICULTY: ★ ★ ★
SOLITUDE: ★ ★

CONFLUENCE OF BIG SPRING BRANCH AND THE CURRENT RIVER

GPS TRAILHEAD COORDINATES: N36° 56.886' W90° 59.469'

DISTANCE AND CONFIGURATION: 3.1-mile figure eight

HIKING TIME: 2 hours

HIGHLIGHTS: Big Spring, Big Spring Branch and confluence with the Current River, Civilian Conservation Corps structures

ELEVATION: 404' at trailhead, 777' at highest point

ACCESS: Open 24/7; no fees or permits required

MAPS: USGS *Big Spring*

FACILITIES: Restrooms, picnic area, campground, and dining lodge in season

WHEELCHAIR ACCESS: Big Spring can be seen from the parking lot, and wheelchair access leads to the northern edge of the spring. The figure eight described here does not have wheelchair access.

COMMENTS: Leashed pets are allowed.

CONTACTS: Ozark National Scenic Riverways, 573-323-4236, nps.gov/ozar

Overview

This hike combines the Spring Branch Trail and a portion of the Stone Ridge Trail. Big Spring is one of those hikes that shouldn't be rushed because you'll want to allow plenty of gawking time. See the largest spring in Missouri and one of the three largest in the United States at a rate of 286 million gallons per day. Big Spring was one of Missouri's first state parks and operated as such from 1924 to 1969, when it became part of a national park.

Route Details

Begin at the dining lodge. Be sure to check out the stone water fountain to the right of the lodge. Then climb the set of stairs next to the water fountain, shortly coming to an overlook. Down on your left, you can see the confluence of the Big Spring Branch with the Current River. The Big Spring flow constitutes enough water to be a river unto itself, but it only flows a few hundred yards before mixing with the Current River.

You'll come to a second stone overlook that gives you a view up and down the Current River. Begin to descend past a park cabin uphill on your right. At the bottom of this hill, you arrive at the Chubb Hollow Trailhead. Take a sharp left and begin following the Current River upstream toward the confluence.

As you hike upstream with the river on your right, you'll follow the base of a bluff on your left and walk down close to river level. You might think you're going to bump your head on the arching bluff over the trail, but there is enough clearance to avoid this unless you're very tall. You'll pass a stone bench and commemorative plaque and then, at 0.5 mile, come to the confluence with the Big Spring flow and a boat dock. The lodge where you began your hike is up on your left.

After passing the boat dock, continue right at a hollowed-out sycamore tree and follow a gravel path across a footbridge. From the bridge, look to your left, and you might see stone steps across the road between two large trees. You'll be using these steps after seeing

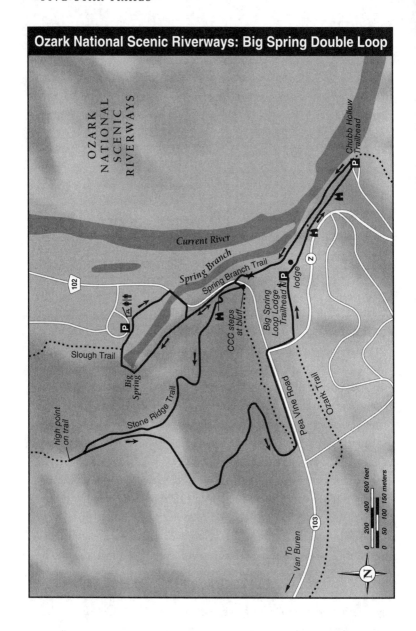

Ozark National Scenic Riverways: Big Spring Double Loop

OZARK NATIONAL SCENIC RIVERWAYS

Chubb Hollow Trailhead

Current River

Spring Branch

Spring Branch Trail

Z

lodge

102

Big Spring Loop Lodge Trailhead

Slough Trail

CCC steps at bluff

Big Spring

Pea Vine Road

Ozark Trail

high point on trail

Stone Ridge Trail

103

To Van Buren

0   200   400   600 feet
0   50   100   150 meters

Big Spring. Cross the footbridge and watch for the gravel path to lead across Pea Vine Road (County Road 60-102). Watch for traffic; this can be a busy place.

Cross the road at 0.7 mile and walk a short distance on the left side of the road, facing opposing traffic. The trail leads up slightly and begins to follow along the base of a beautiful bluff. Follow this bluff all the way to Big Spring. Enjoy this level walk, but watch your step on the stone pavers: they are slippery when wet.

At 0.8 mile, steps come in from your right from a pedestrian bridge that leads to the picnic area. You'll cross another couple of sets of steps along this section, but continue to follow the bluff. It won't be long before you hear the roar of Big Spring. Most tourists will see the spring from the parking lot, but from this route, you'll first see the spring up close and personal.

Arrive at Big Spring at 1.0 mile, a great place to stop and explore. You'll notice caves above the spring. Continue along the path and loop around the spring, snapping photos as you go. Continue to follow the paved walkway around the spring, past an information kiosk and to a picnic pavilion.

Walk across an open field going south with the Big Spring Branch flowing to your right. Cross the bridge over Big Spring Branch, where you can view the power of 286 million gallons flowing from Big Spring.

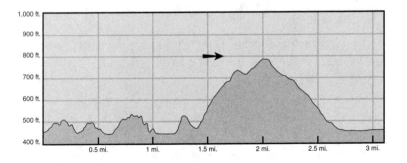

CLOSE-UP VIEW OF BIG SPRING FROM THE TRAIL

After crossing the bridge, walk up the stone steps to the trail at the base of the bluff you followed earlier. This time, turn left and walk with the bluff on your right. For a shorter hike, you could head back to the dining lodge, but you're going to do some climbing now.

The trail ramps back down to the road, and you follow the road a short distance. Watch over your shoulder for oncoming traffic. Shortly, at about 1.5 miles, arrive at the steps between two large trees and turn right to begin your climb. If you have time, check out the historical Civilian Conservation Corps structure up ahead and then return to the steps.

Climb the steps that wind up the bluff. On the way up, you'll pass a small outcrop where you can get a view of the bridge across Big Spring Branch and the picnic area below. This is a pretty good little climb on a path that widens slightly as you go. Just after 1.6 miles, you might notice a smaller trail coming downhill to intersect with this trail, but you're going to continue to walk the larger trail up. One of the benefits of hiking Stone Ridge Trail is getting away from the crowds below. If you pause and stand silently, you might hear the soft roar of Big Spring below.

You may notice another trail on the other side of the ridge you're climbing. You'll come down that trail in just a few minutes. At 2.0 miles, you'll come to a junction with a short spur less than 0.1 mile that continues up to the top of a small knob area on this ridge with views both east and west. The trail continues down the other side, but you're turning around here, returning to the junction, and veering right onto the trail down the right (west) side of the ridge.

Continue down the trail past a deep hollow at 2.5 miles. You'll see evidence of controlled burns in these woods, especially around the bases of large pines. You will see MO 103 below. The trail comes to a sharp right (west) and parallels the highway, with the highway down on your left a short distance. Lots of little rock outcrops are along this section.

The trail continues to descend and arrives at MO 103 at just over 2.7 miles. Turn left (northeast) and follow the highway toward the Big Spring Lodge, where you began your hike. Arrive at MO Z at 2.9 miles and follow it back to the lodge parking area, taking in the interpretive plaques and historical structures along the way.

Arrive back at the Big Spring Lodge parking area and kiosk to complete this 3.1-mile hike.

Nearby Attractions

Skyline Trail is a 3-mile out-and-back located on Skyline Drive just outside of Van Buren. The drive and the hike are a scenic pleasure on your way to Big Spring. You'll probably have the trail to yourself. As you're driving from US 60 on MO 103 South toward Big Spring, turn right onto Skyline Drive and drive 2.9 miles to the trailhead on your left.

Directions

From US 60 in Van Buren, follow MO 103 4 miles to Big Spring. Turn right on MO Z to get to the dining lodge and the beginning of this hike.

Ozark Trail: Rocky Falls to Stegall Mountain Vista

SCENERY: ★ ★ ★ ★ ★
TRAIL CONDITION: ★ ★ ★ ★
CHILDREN: ★ ★ ★
DIFFICULTY: ★ ★ ★ ★
SOLITUDE: ★ ★ ★ ★

OPEN FOREST FLOOR ALONGSIDE THE OZARK TRAIL

GPS TRAILHEAD COORDINATES: N37° 05.692' W91° 12.602'

DISTANCE AND CONFIGURATION: 6.4-mile out-and-back

HIKING TIME: 4 hours

HIGHLIGHTS: Vistas from Stegall Mountain glade peak

ELEVATION: 763' at trailhead, 1,287' at highest point

ACCESS: Open 24/7; no fees or permits required

MAPS: USGS *Stegall Mountain*

FACILITIES: Pit toilets and picnic area

WHEELCHAIR ACCESS: No

COMMENTS: Leashed pets are allowed. Be sure to carry water and snacks on this demanding hike. Once you begin to climb, drainages may be dry.

CONTACTS: Ozark Trail Association, 573-436-0540, ozarktrail.com

Overview

You'll enjoy the expansive views from the glade top of Stegall Mountain. Some of the forests in this area were cut in the early 1900s to provide fuel for a company that smelted low-grade iron ore near Stegall Mountain. Much of the forest has recovered, and controlled burns have helped reestablish the glade areas on and around the mountain. Keep an eye peeled for the collared lizard, a protected species referred to by locals as mountain boomers.

Route Details

Begin at Rocky Falls, a shut-in (a narrow area surrounded by hard rock) with beautifully cascading water when the creeks are running. Step back from the falls and begin walking east at the kiosk. You'll quickly cross Rocky Creek. Rocky Falls might be covered up with people, depending on the weather and day of the week. The trail comes pretty quickly to a great location for camping on your right after crossing the creek.

At 0.5 mile, you'll come to a junction with the Ozark Trail (OT). Turn right (south) and begin walking through some beautiful woods with a small, probably dry, streambed on your left. You'll do some ups and downs along this section but nothing extreme.

Begin a slight climb through beautiful hardwoods around your first mile into the hike. At 1.3 miles, you might find water pockets even in drier times of the year off to your left. Just after 1.5 miles, the trail turns right. Straight looks like an old roadbed, but the roadbed is not the trail. Watch for OT blazes so you don't mistakenly wander up the roadbed and off the trail.

At 1.7 miles, you're into your first serious climb, but it doesn't last long. The trail continues with occasional climbing through drainages. As you top out over a ridge around mile 2.1, you cross an old roadbed. After you cross over the ridge and the roadbed, turn right and begin winding along the other side, climbing higher up the mountain. You may notice an old burned-out wooden bridge at 2.4 miles.

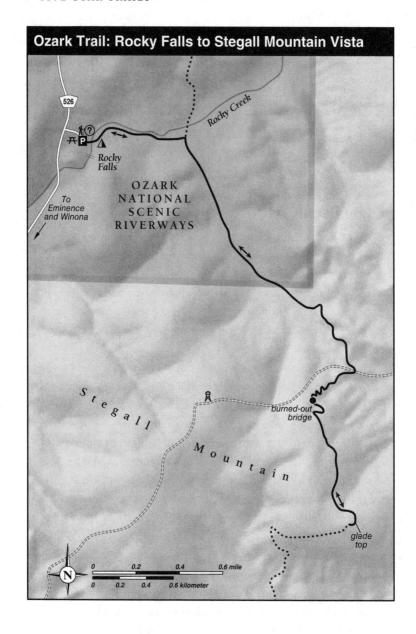

Ozark Trail: Rocky Falls to Stegall Mountain Vista

526

Rocky Creek

Rocky
Falls

To
Eminence
and Winona

OZARK
NATIONAL
SCENIC
RIVERWAYS

Stegall

Mountain

burned-out
bridge

glade
top

N

| 0 | 0.2 | 0.4 | 0.6 mile |
| 0 | 0.2 | 0.4 | 0.6 kilometer |

At almost 2.9 miles, you'll come to a lot of rock outcrops. Follow stacked rock cairns up onto a solid igneous granite bedrock glade that takes you across the top of Stegall Mountain at about 3.2 miles. The OT continues across the top and on to the right (west), but you're going to turn around here and return to Rocky Falls for a 6.4-mile hike. Be careful here. You might feel a strong urge to continue on the OT and walk into the sunset. Turn around and backtrack this trail. You have some easy walking with generally downhill grades back to Rocky Falls.

Nearby Attractions

Ruby's Family Restaurant is a great place to meet local folks and learn about the area. Ruby's serves up good, home-cooked food with friendly service (573-226-3878).

Directions

From Eminence, drive east on MO 106 7.6 miles. Turn right onto MO H and drive 4 miles. Turn left onto MO NN and drive 0.5 mile, then turn right (south) onto Shannon County Road 526. Go 0.3 mile and bear left to the picnic ground and parking area.

From Winona, travel 8.6 miles northeast on MO H. Turn right (east) on MO NN and follow it 0.5 mile, then turn right (south) onto Shannon County Road 526. Go 0.3 mile and bear left to the picnic ground and parking area.

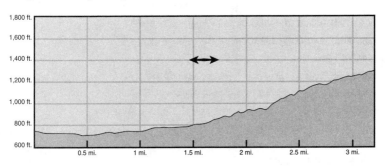

33 # Ozark Trail:
Rocky Falls to Klepzig Mill

SCENERY: ★ ★ ★ ★
TRAIL CONDITION: ★ ★ ★ ★ ★
CHILDREN: ★ ★ ★
DIFFICULTY: ★ ★
SOLITUDE: ★ ★

A REFLECTIVE POOL IN ROCKY CREEK

GPS TRAILHEAD COORDINATES: N37° 05.692' W91° 12.602'
DISTANCE AND CONFIGURATION: 6.6-mile out-and-back
HIKING TIME: 4 hours
HIGHLIGHTS: Rocky Falls, Rocky Creek, and historical Klepzig Mill
ELEVATION: 813' at trailhead, 894' at highest point
ACCESS: Open 24/7; no fees or permits required
MAPS: USGS *Stegall Mountain*
FACILITIES: Pit toilets and picnic area
WHEELCHAIR ACCESS: No
COMMENTS: Leashed pets are allowed.
CONTACTS: Ozark Trail Association, 573-436-0540, ozarktrail.com

Overview

This hike begins at the same trailhead as the Stegall Mountain Trail, but the similarities fade after the first 0.5 mile. Water is abundant on this trail that loosely follows Rocky Creek, arriving at Klepzig Mill, a must-see little turbine mill built in 1928. Elevation changes are not extreme, but prepare to have your breath taken away by Rocky Creek's beauty.

Route Details

The trail begins at a kiosk at Rocky Falls. Be sure to go past the kiosk and see Rocky Falls before returning and beginning your hike. The trail takes you down from the kiosk to cross Rocky Creek. It then goes past a small campsite on your right. At about 0.5 mile, you come to an intersection with the Ozark Trail (OT). Turn left and head north on the OT toward Klepzig Mill.

If you hike in the morning, watch for wildlife. I startled a rafter (flock) of seven turkeys on my first hike of this trail. This section of the OT is open to horses, so watch for evidence of their presence in the middle of the trail. You might want to step around such evidence.

After a climb up and across a high, level section, you'll come down into Denning Hollow and a couple of open grassy areas at 1.4 miles. As you pass the second grassy field, you'll walk about 30 yards on a forest road and then reenter the woods, quickly coming to MO NN. Turn to the right and walk about 40 yards on the road before turning left (northwest) and entering back onto the trail.

Pass through a scrubby section with lots of pine and then a cedar grove with some briars due to the lack of a canopy. This could easily be overgrown, but it's obvious that regular maintenance is occurring. Compliments to the Ozark Trail Association on the good work! My legs thank you.

At 2.1 miles, turn left onto an old roadbed alongside Rocky Creek. You'll come to what I like to call a PUD (pointless up and down). The trail climbs to a rocky crag and then comes down to arrive

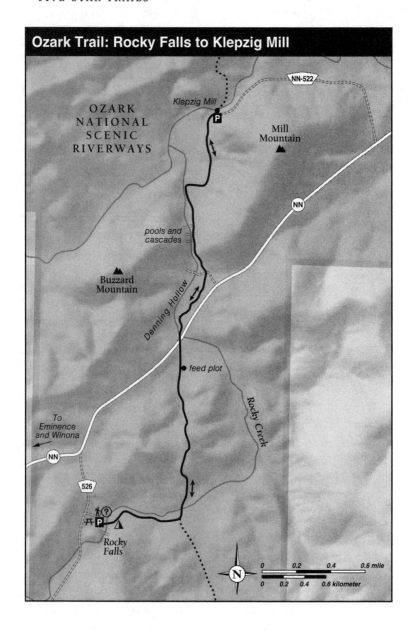

Ozark Trail: Rocky Falls to Klepzig Mill

OZARK
NATIONAL
SCENIC
RIVERWAYS

OZARK NATIONAL SCENIC RIVERWAYS

NN-522

Klepzig Mill

Mill
Mountain

NN

pools and
cascades

Buzzard
Mountain

Denning Hollow

feed plot

Rocky Creek

To
Eminence
and Winona

NN

526

Rocky
Falls

N

| 0 | 0.2 | 0.4 | 0.6 mile |
| 0 | 0.2 | 0.4 | 0.6 kilometer |

at a beautiful section of Rocky Creek. This area, with its cascades and pools, is a place you'll want to hang out for a while. I spent a wonderful hour with my camera here on my first hike through.

After leaving Rocky Creek, you'll see another grassy area as the trail skirts around it on the right with views across the field to tree-covered hills on the other side.

You'll arrive at Klepzig Mill at 3.2 miles. Spend some time exploring the Klepzig Mill and Rocky Creek. The son of a German immigrant, Walter Klepzig built this turbine mill in 1928. Spend some time checking out his handiwork. He was frugal and industrious. His little mill has stood the test of time sitting here next to Rocky Creek.

After exploring the mill, turn around and head back to Rocky Falls. For a shorter hike, place a shuttle vehicle here, but then you'd miss seeing those beautiful Rocky Creek cascades and pools a second time.

Nearby Attractions

Ruby's Family Restaurant is a great place to meet local folks and learn about the area. Ruby's serves up good, home-cooked food with friendly service (573-226-3878).

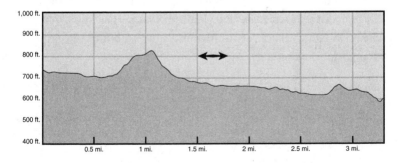

KLEPZIG MILL

Directions

From Eminence, drive east on MO 106 7.6 miles. Turn right onto MO H and drive 4 miles. Turn left onto MO NN and drive 0.5 mile, then turn right (south) onto Shannon County Road 526. Go 0.3 mile and bear left to the picnic ground and parking area.

From Winona, travel 8.6 miles northeast on MO H. Turn right (east) on MO NN and follow it 0.5 mile, then turn right (south) onto Shannon County Road 526. Go 0.3 mile and bear left to the picnic ground and parking area.

Ozark Trail:
Current River Vista at Owls Bend

SCENERY: ★ ★ ★ ★
TRAIL CONDITION: ★ ★ ★ ★ ★
CHILDREN: ★ ★ ★ ★
DIFFICULTY: ★ ★
SOLITUDE: ★ ★ ★

HIKER-DOG TAKES A BREAK ON A CURRENT RIVER BLUFF.

GPS TRAILHEAD COORDINATES: N37° 11.087' W91° 10.515'

DISTANCE AND CONFIGURATION: 3.4-mile out-and-back

HIKING TIME: 2 hours

HIGHLIGHTS: Current River views from high above blufflines

ELEVATION: 570' at trailhead, 761' at highest point

ACCESS: Open 24/7; no fees or permits required

MAPS: USGS *Powder Mill Ferry*

FACILITIES: Restrooms and water are available during warmer seasons at the Powder Mill Campground.

WHEELCHAIR ACCESS: No

COMMENTS: Leashed pets are allowed.

CONTACTS: Ozark Trail Association, 573-436-0540, ozarktrail.com

Ozark Trail: Current River Vista at Owls Bend

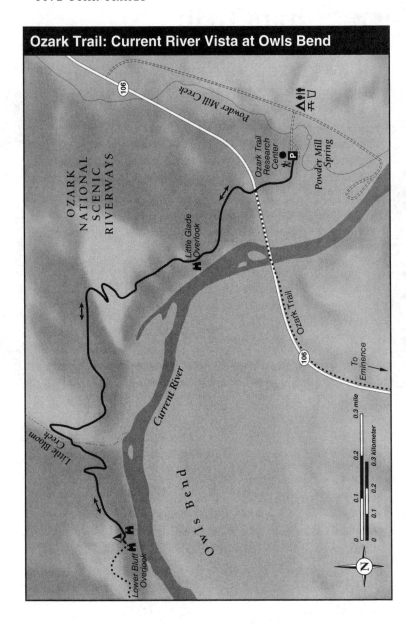

Overview

This route takes you to a special view of the Current River and Owls Bend from high on a bluff. Several nice viewing spots are along the bluff with a campsite close by. This hike also gives you a chance to visit the Ozark Trail Research Center at the trailhead.

Route Details

Begin at the Ozark Trail Research Center, walking to the left side of the front of the building. The trail goes a short distance through thick bottomland before crossing MO 106. After crossing the highway, the trail links with the Ozark Trail, going straight and north on top of bluffs. Don't turn left at the Current River Bridge because that will take you south on the Ozark Trail.

Walk to the east side of the Current River Bridge, immediately climbing with nice views down to the river valley. After a few switchbacks, you'll come to a small grassy glade with views down to the Current River at Owls Bend. Continue up on the main trail, moving away from the river and crossing a couple of small creeks. The second creek is Little Bloom Creek and may contain water depending on the season.

Coming out of the Bloom Creek drainage, the trail makes a couple of long switchbacks up and then tops out at 1.6 miles. You'll pass a small campsite on your right and then come to a short spur trail that

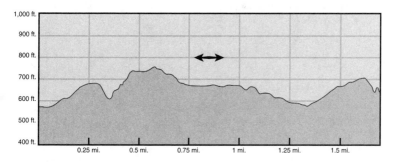

takes you to a bluff overlook with expansive views of the Current River. This is a great place to take a break and enjoy the views. The main trail then goes another 15 yards, where you can get a nice view of the bluff-line you were just standing on. This is where you'll turn around and backtrack to the Ozark Trail Research Center for a 3.4-mile hike.

Nearby Attractions

Ozark Trail Research Center is rarely open but serves as a hub for the volunteer efforts of the Ozark Trail Association (573-436-0540; ozarktrail.com).

Powder Mill Campground is beautifully situated on the Current River (877-444-6777; nps.gov/ozar/planyourvisit/camping.htm). Campsites have a picnic table, fire pit, and access to a restroom.

Directions

From Eminence, drive east on MO 106 13 miles. Turn right onto County Road 106-531 and drive 0.5 mile to the Ozark Trail Research Center on your right. Parking is available. The trailhead kiosk is to the left (west) of the research center, and the trail begins behind the building.

Ozark National Scenic Riverways: Powder Mill to Blue Spring on the Current River

SCENERY: ★ ★ ★ ★ ★
TRAIL CONDITION: ★ ★ ★
CHILDREN: ★ ★ ★ ★
DIFFICULTY: ★ ★
SOLITUDE: ★ ★ ★

BLUE SPRING ON THE CURRENT RIVER

GPS TRAILHEAD COORDINATES: N37° 10.852' W91° 10.399'

DISTANCE AND CONFIGURATION: 3-mile out-and-back

HIKING TIME: 2 hours

HIGHLIGHTS: Current River views, Blue Spring and observation decks, and Blue Spring Branch

ELEVATION: 525' at trailhead, 562' at highest point

ACCESS: Open 24/7; no fees or permits required

MAPS: USGS *Powder Mill*

FACILITIES: Campground with water and restroom available during warmer seasons

WHEELCHAIR ACCESS: No

COMMENTS: Leashed pets are allowed.

CONTACTS: Ozark National Scenic Riverways, 573-323-4236, nps.gov/ozar

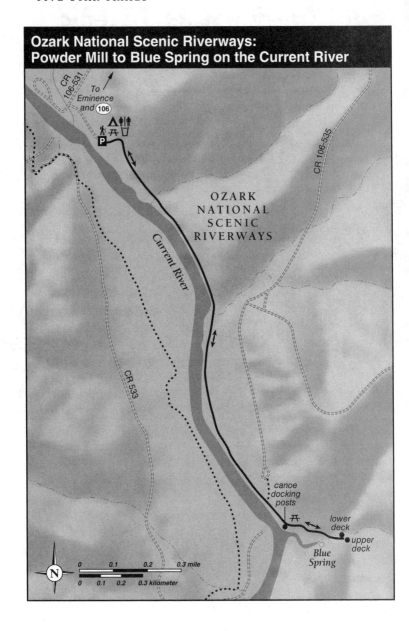

Ozark National Scenic Riverways:
Powder Mill to Blue Spring on the Current River

Overview

The Osage Indians were said to have called it Spring of the Summer Sky. Dissolved limestone and dolomite, combined with the 310-foot depth of the spring, gives it that sky-blue hue. The National Park Service brochure illustrates the depth of the spring by saying you could put the Statue of Liberty down into Blue Spring and the torch would be 5 feet below the surface.

Blue Spring delivers 90 million gallons of water into the Current River each day. The aquatic plants in the branch just below the surface of the spring impart a rich, green color, and leaves seem to float above the surface due to the clarity of the water. Visiting Blue Spring by trail is the best way to absorb and appreciate its beauty.

Route Details

The route is pretty straight ahead and level along the Current River to Blue Spring. The trail begins at the southeast corner of the Powder Mill Campground next to a circle drive. After hiking into the woods, you'll come quickly next to the Current River, hiking downstream with the river on your right side. You'll follow alongside the Current River all the way to Blue Spring.

Walk a short distance, and you'll cross a small footbridge. Shortly after the bridge, you'll see some giant sycamore trees that thrive next

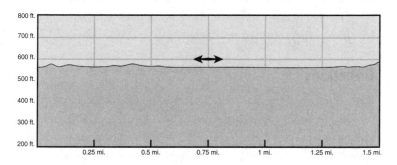

to water. You might notice some debris up in the trees, indicating how high water levels sometimes reach. You may encounter some narrow trail tread, as water sometimes washes out parts of the footpath.

This is a pretty easy trail, but several times on this path next to the river, you'll walk through sandy sections that feel like they're trying to swallow your feet. At 1.2 miles, come to a spur to the left that takes you to a parking area and restrooms. Keep going straight past a sign that says you are entering the Blue Spring area. A short distance more and you come to a metal lid and spur down to the river to a boat docking spot. After this spur, walk up a small branch that is flowing from the spring.

Arrive at Blue Spring at 1.5 miles. Beautiful stonework, as well as two viewing decks, are around the spring. After spending some time on the boardwalks and relaxing next to the spring, return by the same route to complete this 3-mile hike.

Nearby Attractions

Ozark Trail Research Center is rarely open but serves as a hub for the volunteer efforts of the Ozark Trail Association (573-436-0540; ozarktrail.com).

Powder Mill Campground is beautifully situated on the Current River (877-444-6777; nps.gov/ozar/planyourvisit/camping.htm). Campsites have a picnic table, fire pit, and access to a restroom.

Eminence provides food and lodging options and a small town feel. Don't expect businesses to be open late or at odd hours.

Directions

From Eminence, drive east on MO 106 14 miles. Turn right (south) on County Road 106-531 and watch for the Powder Mill Campground and parking area on the left. You'll pass the entrance to the Ozark Trail Research Center on the right just before arriving at the Powder Mill Campground.

Johnson's Shut-Ins
State Park: Shut-Ins Trail

SCENERY: ★ ★ ★ ★ ★
TRAIL CONDITION: ★ ★ ★ ★ ★
CHILDREN: ★ ★ ★ ★
DIFFICULTY: ★ ★ ★
SOLITUDE: ★ ★ ★

EAST FORK BLACK RIVER

GPS TRAILHEAD COORDINATES: N37° 32.401' W90° 50.612'

DISTANCE AND CONFIGURATION: 2.5-mile loop

HIKING TIME: 2 hours

HIGHLIGHTS: Vistas down across the East Fork Black River and intricate rock formations

ELEVATION: 838' at trailhead, 978' at highest point

ACCESS: March–Wednesday before Memorial Day and Labor Day–October: Daily, 8 a.m.–6 p.m.; Thursday before Memorial Day–Labor Day: Daily, 8 a.m.–7 p.m.; November–February: Daily, 8 a.m.–4 p.m.; no fees or permits required

MAPS: USGS *Johnson Shut-Ins*

FACILITIES: Restrooms and water during the warmer seasons. Campsites and picnic areas are available.

WHEELCHAIR ACCESS: Access on the paved path and boardwalk to where the stairs begin

COMMENTS: No pets allowed on this trail. Wheelchair access allows visitors to see a section of the East Fork Black River.

CONTACTS: Johnson's Shut-Ins State Park, 573-546-2450, mostateparks.com/park /johnsons-shut-ins-state-park

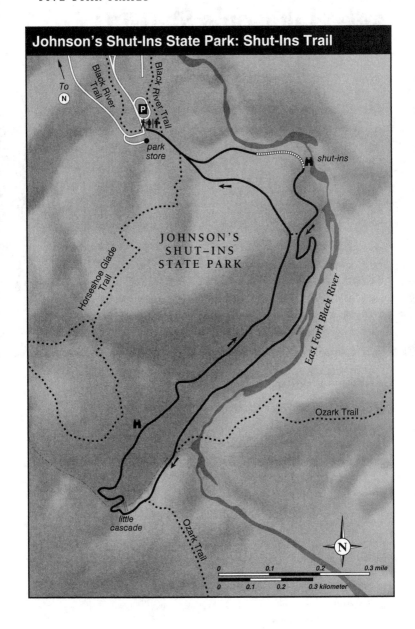

Johnson's Shut-Ins State Park: Shut-Ins Trail

To N

Black River Trail

Black River Trail

P

park store

JOHNSON'S SHUT–INS STATE PARK

Horseshoe Glade Trail

shut-ins

East Fork Black River

Ozark Trail

little cascade

Ozark Trail

N

| 0 | 0.1 | 0.2 | 0.3 mile |
| 0 | 0.1 | 0.2 | 0.3 kilometer |

Overview

You'll find yourself thinking, "I'm so glad that this trail goes exactly where it goes." The boardwalk and stairs are engineering feats of the man-made type and provide access to views of Mother Nature's ongoing hydraulics and engineering at work, carving rocky riverbeds below.

Route Details

Begin on the left side of the ranger station at the south end of the parking for the day-use area. The first part of this trail is paved and wheelchair accessible. Pretty quickly, you'll pass a junction with the Horseshoe Glade Trail to the right, marked with orange blazes. To the left is a solar-powered restroom. Continue straight on the paved trail, following the blue blazes.

At 0.1 mile, pass another junction on the right where this loop trail returns, but continue straight on the paved trail. You'll pass several spurs down to the edge of East Fork Black River. The trail begins to follow a railed boardwalk. The river is flowing into the shut-ins (a narrow part of the river surrounded by hard rock) as you're hiking downstream. Maybe it's just me, but it looked like the river was flowing uphill where the water enters the deep rock that forms these shut-ins.

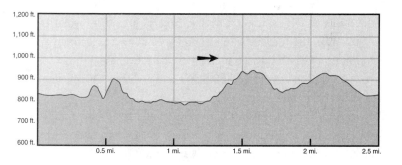

EAST FORK BLACK RIVER FLOWING THROUGH MASSIVE BOULDERS

You'll climb a series of nice stairs to an overlook with a view of the river's clear, blue water. Get that camera out and rest your legs. At 0.5 mile, the trail turns to dirt and goes up to a steep bluff and continues to climb through a mature cedar forest. You'll come back down toward the river level at 0.8 mile and probably see evidence of occasional flooding.

After a short visit to the river, the trail moves away from the water and into a pine grove. At 1.2 miles, you'll pass a campsite and junction with a white connector Ozark Trail (OT) spur. You'll continue following blue blazes. You'll also see OT signs in this section.

Cross a small stream, and then bear right. Shortly, the OT veers left, but you veer right following the blue blazes on the Shut-Ins Trail. You're following the same stream you crossed earlier. This is a visual treat, especially if there's water. Cross the drainage you've been walking next to at 1.4 miles and immediately begin hiking up at a good clip.

The trail reaches a wet-season waterfall. At the top of the cascades and stream you've been following, the trail takes a sharp right away from the drainage and continues through small oak cedar forest.

Watch for a sharp left following the blue blazes into a rocky cedar grove at almost 1.5 miles. You'll find yourself walking on top of the world in this small mixed-cedar glade area.

You'll come to a narrow rocky outcrop at 1.7 miles, and work your way downhill with the river far away on your right. The trail veers left and crosses a small moss-covered drainage. As you walk along, enjoy the soft roar of the East Fork Black River far below.

At 2.0 miles, turn left onto an old rocky roadbed. Continue down the roadbed for about 0.4 mile, and then it connects with the paved route where you began your hike. Backtrack to the parking lot to complete this 2.5-mile hike.

Nearby Attractions

Arcadia Academy and Three Abbey Kitchen provide a variety of bed-and-breakfast rooms, elegant dining, and a gift shop surrounded by historical architecture (314-960-1983; arcadiavalleyacademy.com).

Directions

From Ironton, drive north on MO 21 4.3 miles. Turn left to stay on MO 21 N (straight turns into MO NN). After turning left, continue 0.5 mile and turn left onto MO N. Follow MO N to the southeast for 12.8 miles and turn left into Johnson's Shut-Ins State Park. Pass the visitor center on your right and continue driving all the way back to the ranger station at the south end of the park where the trail begins.

Taum Sauk Mountain
State Park: Mina Sauk Falls Trail

SCENERY: ★ ★ ★ ★ ★
TRAIL CONDITION: ★ ★ ★ ★ ★
CHILDREN: ★ ★ ★ ★
DIFFICULTY: ★ ★ ★
SOLITUDE: ★ ★ ★

EARLY MORNING ON TAUM SAUK MOUNTAIN AT THE HIGHEST POINT IN MISSOURI

GPS TRAILHEAD COORDINATES: N37° 34.363' W90° 43.696'

DISTANCE AND CONFIGURATION: 3.2-mile balloon

HIKING TIME: 2.5 hours

HIGHLIGHTS: High point of Missouri, Mina Sauk Falls, and creek above the falls

ELEVATION: 1,765' at trailhead, 1,772' at highest point

ACCESS: Open 24/7; no fees or permits required

MAPS: USGS *Ironton*

FACILITIES: Restrooms year-round and water during the warmer seasons

WHEELCHAIR ACCESS: The first 0.2 mile from the trailhead to the Missouri high point is wheelchair accessible. From there, the trail is a dirt and rock path.

COMMENTS: Leashed pets are allowed.

CONTACTS: Taum Sauk Mountain State Park, 573-546-2450, mostateparks.com/park /taum-sauk-mountain-state-park

Overview

This trail visits Missouri's highest point in elevation with a wheelchair-accessible paved path. From there, a loop trail skirts rocky bluffs and high ridge forests. You'll also pass by the tallest waterfall in Missouri, the 132-foot-tall Mina Sauk Falls. You'll have the option of hiking to the bottom of the falls for a better look.

Legends say that the Piankashaw's tribal leader, Taum Sauk, became enraged when his daughter, Mina Sauk, fell in love with an Osage warrior. The warrior was executed by being thrown down the mountain. Mina Sauk was grief-stricken and threw herself down the mountain to the rocks below. The Great Spirit was not pleased, and the mountain trembled, displacing rocks and causing water to flow down the mountainside as Mina Sauk Falls.

Route Details

Begin on a paved path next to a covered pavilion. Pass restrooms on your right and continue, following orange blazes. Come to a junction where the paved path goes to your left to the Missouri high point at 0.2 mile. You'll find a marble plaque, bench, and trail register. You'll see a U.S. Geological Survey marker that states the elevation as 1,772 feet.

Backtrack a short distance and turn left (southwest) to continue with the main route, arriving at a junction at 0.3 mile. Here, you'll find a sign and trail register cards. Turn right and begin the loop hike on a level and easy trail. The rugged parts come later, so wear some sturdy shoes.

You'll come to rocky sections at 0.8 mile, where the view opens up to mountains across a valley. At 1.0 mile, you come to a spectacular overlook, a great photo spot and a place to hang out for a while. The trail then goes steeply down a rocky section and continues to descend slightly as it veers to the right.

Continuing around the loop at 1.3 miles, the trail levels out, and you'll hear the sounds of water if the cascades of Mina Sauk Falls are running. You'll come to a junction with the Ozark Trail (OT) and

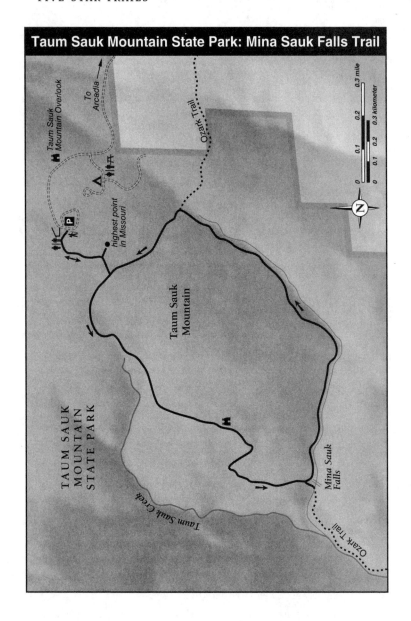

Taum Sauk Mountain State Park: Mina Sauk Falls Trail

a sign indicating that the falls are just ahead. To get the best view of Mina Sauk Falls, you'll need to turn right and take the first couple of hundred rocky feet on the trail to the base of the falls. Because the falls are located on the west side of the mountain, you might get a good photo if you get an early start, even on bright, sunny days.

Backtrack on the OT up to the loop trail junction and then turn right (southeast). The trail begins to follow the stream that feeds Mina Sauk Falls. This is a beautiful walk. Boulders along this stream appear to be placed by a master artist. The trail gradient decreases as you go farther next to the creek. At 2.5 miles, come to another junction where the OT leaves and turn left (northwest) to continue your loop. From here, it's only about 0.5 mile back to the trailhead.

You'll come back to the intersection that completes the loop at 2.8 miles. Turn right onto the paved trail and return to the trailhead, passing the Missouri high point spur on your right and completing this 3.2-mile trail.

Nearby Attractions

Arcadia Academy and Three Abbey Kitchen provide a variety of bed-and-breakfast rooms, elegant dining, and a gift shop surrounded by historical architecture (314-960-1983; arcadiavalleyacademy.com).

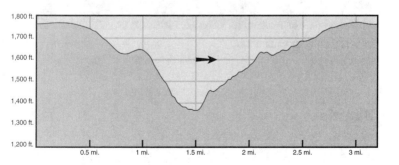

CASCADE ON TAUM SAUK CREEK

Directions

From Arcadia, south of Ironton, drive south on MO 72/MO 21 4.2 miles. Turn right on MO CC and drive 3.2 miles to Taum Sauk Mountain; continue another 0.7 mile, passing the campground entrance on your left and going straight to the trailhead.

Elephant Rocks State Park:
Braille Trail and Engine House

SCENERY: ★ ★ ★ ★
TRAIL CONDITION: ★ ★ ★ ★ ★
CHILDREN: ★ ★ ★ ★
DIFFICULTY: ★
SOLITUDE: ★

A YOUNG CHILD EXPLORES ELEPHANT ROCKS.

GPS TRAILHEAD COORDINATES: N37° 39.186' W90° 41.335'

DISTANCE AND CONFIGURATION: 1.1-mile loop

HIKING TIME: 1.5 hours

HIGHLIGHTS: Massive elephant-shaped granite rocks and historical mining sites

ELEVATION: 1,192' at trailhead, 1,265' at highest point

ACCESS: April–October: Daily, 8 a.m.–8 p.m.; November–March: Daily, 8 a.m.–5 p.m.; no fees or permits required

MAPS: USGS *Graniteville*

FACILITIES: Restrooms and water available during the warmer seasons

WHEELCHAIR ACCESS: Yes. Interpretive signs include Braille text.

COMMENTS: Leashed pets allowed. Rock-climbing equipment is not to be used in the park, although scrambling is encouraged. Camping is not available in the park.

CONTACTS: Elephant Rocks State Park, 573-546-3454, mostateparks.com/park /elephant-rocks-state-park

Elephant Rocks State Park: Braille Trail and Engine House

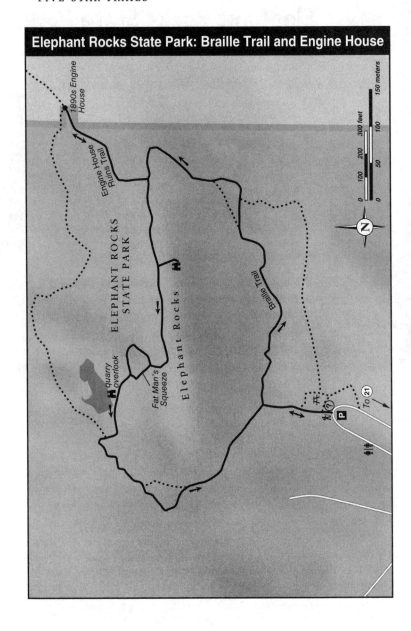

Overview

Everything about this trail says "accessibility." Elephant Rocks State Park is located right on MO 21. The large, covered kiosk is inviting and includes information brochures and maps of the area. Multiple restrooms are available with wheelchair accessibility. Best of all, the paved trail with print and Braille interpretive signs circles a beautiful collection of massive, smooth-surfaced boulders and sharp-edged granite boulder piles. It's like a rock playground for all ages.

If you have time for exploring, you might want to get an overview by doing the loop and then going back and letting your interests be your guide. There's no danger of getting lost in this compact area.

This trail includes signs with Braille for the visually impaired. It is the shortest trail I review in this trail guide, but you can walk your legs off exploring every nook and cranny of this beautiful site that invites you to leave the paved route and crawl among the boulders.

Route Details

This hike covers the Braille Trail that begins under the kiosk at the north side of the parking lot. There are several route options for this trail, but this description follows the handicapped-accessible trail that circles the Elephant Rocks, with many options for exploring. The trail is marked with red blazes. Turn right and begin the loop going counterclockwise.

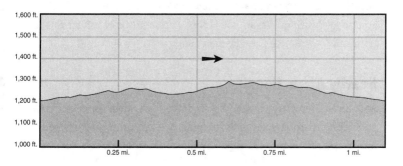

At 0.4 mile, there is a junction with a trail marked in blue blazes. Turn right and walk about 430 feet on a surface not wheelchair accessible to the Engine House ruins. During the 1890s, trains were maintained and repaired by the Iron Mountain and Southern Railway in this structure. You can see where the train tracks go right into the building. After looking around, head back the way you came.

Once back to the main trail, turn right and continue on the wheelchair-accessible loop. There are boulders to explore all along the trail. At 0.6 mile, turn left to walk up to an overlook that isn't wheelchair accessible. Notice the native stone used to make this scenic overlook. This is close to the high point in the park at 1,270 feet and a good place to access some of the massive elephant-shaped rocks. Follow the path back down to the main trail and continue on the loop to the left.

At 0.7 mile, come to Fat Man's Squeeze. Take this as a little out-and-back spur so you can squeeze through twice and then continue on the main trail. You might feel like you're down in a slot canyon as you slip through the pressing boulders. The kids will love this!

Continuing on the loop, you'll quickly arrive at a granite quarry overlook, and then at a trail junction that offers another route to the Engine House. Since you took the earlier spur to see this, continue on the paved loop to the left.

At 0.9 mile, the trail splits; take the right-hand route because it's longer and offers a contrasting view of surrounding woods with large boulders strewn about. At just over a mile, arrive back at the junction where you began your loop. Turn right and return to the trailhead to complete this 1.1-mile hike.

Nearby Attractions

Arcadia Academy and Three Abbey Kitchen provide a variety of bed-and-breakfast rooms, elegant dining, and a gift shop surrounded by historical architecture (314-960-1983; arcadiavalleyacademy.com).

LEASHED DOGS ARE WELCOME ON THE BRAILLE TRAIL.

Shepherd Mountain Inn is a casual but clean motel adjacent to Baylee Jo's BBQ, a good place for a posthike meal (573-546-7418; shepherdmtninn.com).

Directions

From Ironton, drive north on MO 21 4.6 miles. Turn left to stay on MO 21 North (MO NN continues straight). Continue on MO 21 1.6 miles to the entrance to Elephant Rocks State Park on the right. The covered trailhead kiosk is at the north end of the long parking lot.

**Pickle Springs
Natural Area:**

Trail Through Time

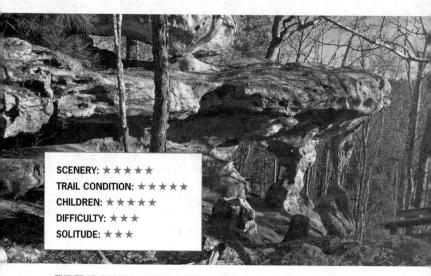

SCENERY: ★ ★ ★ ★ ★
TRAIL CONDITION: ★ ★ ★ ★ ★
CHILDREN: ★ ★ ★ ★ ★
DIFFICULTY: ★ ★ ★
SOLITUDE: ★ ★ ★

THE TRAIL PASSES THROUGH DOUBLE ARCH.

GPS TRAILHEAD COORDINATES: N37° 48.078' W90° 18.093'

DISTANCE AND CONFIGURATION: 2-mile loop

HIKING TIME: 1.5 hours

HIGHLIGHTS: Geological features with unusual rock formations, water features, and plant and animal diversity

ELEVATION: 1,062' at trailhead, 1,062' at highest point, 877' at lowest point

ACCESS: Open 24/7; no fees or permits required

MAPS: USGS *Sprott*

FACILITIES: None

WHEELCHAIR ACCESS: No

COMMENTS: Leashed pets are allowed. An optional easy hike would be an out-and-back to the Double Arch. This would give you a short 0.8-mile hike with a slight climb on the return portion.

CONTACTS: Missouri Department of Conservation, Southeast Regional Office, 573-290-5730, nature.mdc.mo.gov/discover-nature/places/pickle-springs

Overview

Pickle Springs Natural Area is a pure pleasure to walk, with beauty in every step. You'll find a geological wonderland with a variety of rock formations, a double arch, hoodoos, and water features inside cool box canyons. Biological diversity abounds in this natural area, making it a must-see and worthy of repeated visits in every season.

Pickle Springs and Creek get their names from the original owner of the area dating back to 1848. William Pickle moved from England to the United States in 1842. Local legend has it that he was shot by renegades after the Civil War.

Route Details

The trailhead is on the east side of the parking lot. It's a short walk to the junction with the loop trail and an informational kiosk. The kiosk indicates this trail is one way, so turn left and hike north. You won't see any trail blazes, but there are occasional signs along the path.

At just under 0.2 mile, take a sharp right and walk into The Slot, where you'll have the feeling of being deep in a slot canyon. Watch for the cave within The Slot, and other interesting rock formations. After coming out of The Slot, you'll pass a moss-covered bluff and make a gradual descent toward the Double Arch, arriving at 0.4 mile. This is an iconic feature of the area. A stairwell leads down to this unusual formation, walking you right through the arches that hold a shelf of sandstone and a large, rounded boulder on top.

A short distance down the trail leads you to the Keyhole, a set of massive boulders stacked so that you can stoop down and slip through. Leaving the Keyhole behind, you'll come to a hoodoo called Terrapin Rock at 0.5 mile. You're probably wondering if this trail has scenic features every tenth of a mile. The answer is yes!

Just past Terrapin Rock, you may see evidence of a shortcut. Please don't take it. Continue down the trail and take the switch-back where the tread leads. Because of heavy use, there are a couple of spots where shortcuts have been taken around switchbacks.

Pickle Springs Natural Area: Trail Through Time

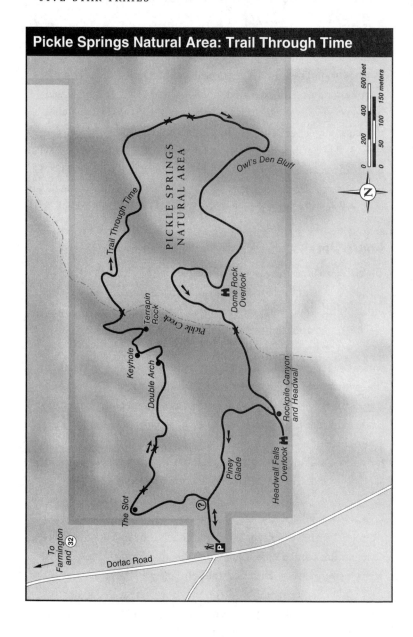

These shortcuts cause erosion and are an eyesore on this pristine environment.

Cross Pickle Creek on a small bridge at 0.6 mile. This is a great spot for relaxing and enjoying cascading water or watching for wildlife.

At 0.9 mile, come to a pair of small bridges that do a zigzag across Bone Creek close to a small waterfall. Soon afterward, you'll come to Owl's Den Bluff with a bench placed perfectly for viewing the area. Walking along this bluff might give you a drippy experience, but you'll get a close-up view of the lush ferns and mosses along its base. This is a pretty place to hang out for a while.

You'll come to Dome Rock Overlook at 1.4 miles. Be careful next to these steep drop-offs, but enjoy the views into the Pickle Creek drainage from this massive rock formation. Follow the direction of arrows that lead you off the dome to the north.

The trail veers left to come alongside Pickle Creek and then crosses it a second time just below a 3-foot waterfall at 1.5 miles. A sign indicates this is Pickle Springs. As you approach the bridge, be sure to pause and look back at the Dome Rock formation where you were standing a few minutes before. You can now see the randomly placed crevices and small caves scattered over its rock face.

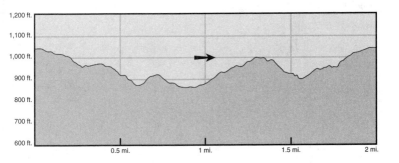

Just after 1.6 miles, arrive at Rockpile Canyon, a beautiful, high bluff with huge piles of rocks that have been displaced from the canyon walls over the years. There's also an overlook at Headwall Falls another 50 feet down the trail. Both are beautiful scenic features. How's my earlier statement holding up about finding something beautiful every tenth of a mile?

As you hike up and out of this little canyon, walk through Piney Glade and then arrive back at the junction where you started your loop earlier. Turn left and head back to the trailhead to complete this 2-mile hike.

Nearby Attractions

Beautiful Hawn State Park, home to Pickle Creek and towering pine forests, has camping with electric hookups, picnic areas, restrooms, and hiking trails (573-883-3603; mostateparks.com/park/hawn-state-park).

Directions

From the junction of MO 32 and Washington Street/MO D in Farmington, travel east on MO 32 4.6 miles, then turn right (east) on MO AA. Follow MO AA east 1.7 miles to Dorlac Road (gravel). Turn left (north) onto Dorlac Road and drive 0.4 mile to the parking lot on the right (east) side.

40 Hawn State Park:

Pickle Creek and Whispering Pines
North Loop

CASCADES IN PICKLE CREEK

GPS TRAILHEAD COORDINATES: N37° 49.804' W90° 13.906'

DISTANCE AND CONFIGURATION: 6.5-mile loop

HIKING TIME: 4.5 hours

HIGHLIGHTS: Pickle Creek cascades, pine forests, rocky ridges, and high mountain vistas

ELEVATION: 639' at trailhead, 1,009' at highest point

ACCESS: March 15–November 14: Daily, 7:30 a.m.–9 p.m.; November 15–March 14: Daily, 7:30 a.m.–sunset; no fees or permits required

MAPS: USGS *Coffman*

FACILITIES: Restrooms, pavilion, and picnic area at trailhead

WHEELCHAIR ACCESS: No

COMMENTS: Leashed pets are allowed. An optional short hike would be the Pickle Creek section for a 1.6-mile out-and-back.

CONTACTS: Hawn State Park, 573-883-3603, mostateparks.com/park/hawn-state-park

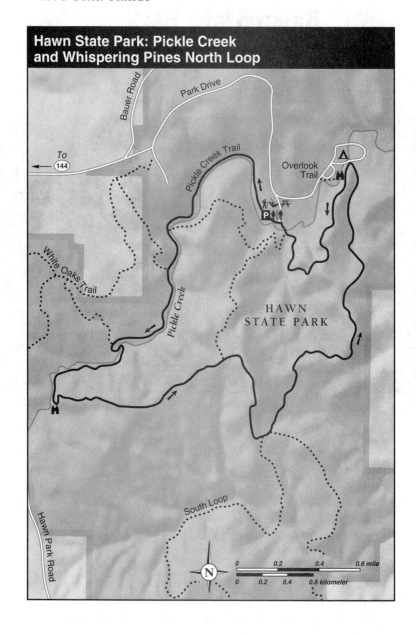

Hawn State Park: Pickle Creek and Whispering Pines North Loop

Bauer Road

Park Drive

To 144

Pickle Creek Trail

Overlook Trail

White Oaks Trail

Pickle Creek

Pickle Creek

HAWN STATE PARK

South Loop

Hawn Park Road

N

| 0 | 0.2 | 0.4 | 0.6 mile |

| 0 | 0.2 | 0.4 | 0.6 kilometer |

Overview

Get warmed up on the rocky and picturesque Pickle Creek before launching into a long loop through majestic pine forests, across high mountain ridges and rocky ledges. You'll see the effects of forest management and see some large pines and hardwoods on the North Loop of Whispering Pines Trail.

Route Details

Begin at the Pickle Creek Trailhead on the northwest side of the parking area. You'll walk through the picnic area following green blazes. The trail quickly comes alongside Pickle Creek on your left.

You may see evidence of prescribed burns up on your right and away from the creek. Tree size and health are enhanced if the burns are done correctly to replicate the action of natural fires. Prescribed burns encourage new pine growth, help keep the forest floor more open, and stimulate wildlife in the area. Later in this hike, you'll be able to compare areas that are routinely burned with areas that are not.

Continuing up the creek, you may see debris from occasional high creek levels. It's surprising to see limbs and leaves suspended high overhead from flooding. Stop occasionally and enjoy pools and cascades, which are plentiful along this section.

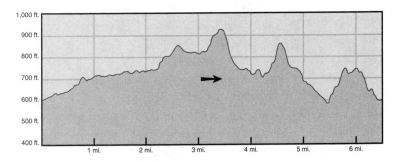

At 0.7 mile, you'll get a nice view down onto the creek from a glade area. At 1.0 mile, pass a connector trail to White Oaks Trail on your right, but keep going south, following the creek trail and green blazes. The character of Pickle Creek changes from a lively to a more tranquil stream with fewer rocks and a sandier bottom.

As you progress past 1.4 miles, you'll see evidence that controlled burns are benefiting this pine forest. To the right of the trail, the forest is more open. Between the trail and Pickle Creek, where controlled burns do not occur, there is more undergrowth.

You'll come to a second connector trail at 1.6 miles into the hike. Veer left after crossing a small creek that is a tributary to Pickle Creek. You're now following red blazes for the North Loop of Whispering Pines Trail. Shortly you'll come to Pickle Creek and cross before veering right to follow Pickle Creek west, with the creek on your right. This is easy walking with few ups and downs. The trail begins to move away from the creek at about 2.2 miles and switchbacks up to a higher rocky outcrop, where you get a view down on the creek.

Once on top of this ridge, you're almost 100 feet higher above the creek than you were a few minutes ago. You'll make good time on the trail along this ridge traveling east for a while. If a breeze is passing over this ridge, you'll see why the trail is called Whispering Pines.

Being among tall pines on this ridge reminds me of a couple of ice storms from my childhood. During the night, you'd hear what sounded like cannon booms. The next day, you'd see half a pine tree standing with the upper half lying on the ground next to the tree. Pine needles hold lots of ice, so ice storms can be devastating to a pine forest.

At 3.1 miles, come to another connector trail to your left, marked in white blazes. You're going straight (northeast) here, following the red blazes of Whispering Pines Trail North Loop. The trail turns to the right (south) and climbs over a 1,000-foot-high ridge at 3.4 miles with some nice views during fall and winter, when leaves are off the trees. You'll then descend the southern side of this ridge through thick undergrowth. Watch for the red blazes and enjoy the view as you come down off this ridge.

You'll arrive at the junction with the South Loop marked in blue blazes to the right at 3.7 miles. Stay straight (east) with the red blazes and the North Loop. This little portion of trail is shared by both loops. You quickly come to another junction that indicates to turn left (north) and continue on the North Loop marked in red blazes. Compliments to Hawn State Park for the good signage and trail blazes.

You'll climb another little mountain that feels like the toughest climb of the day, topping out at about 4.3 miles—a nice place for a break. The trail begins a mile-long gradual descent to Pickle Creek. Follow a small stream on your right that eventually feeds into Pickle Creek.

Arrive next to Pickle Creek again at 5.4 miles, and climb to a rock outcrop. I paused here with my dog, Hiker-dog, and was impressed with how she seemed to appreciate the view down into Pickle Creek Valley. Then I realized she was just watching a squirrel. She's a good dog, but all dog!

There's still a little more climbing ahead, and then the trail begins to trend downhill overall to the end of the trail at 6.5 miles, coming out at the Whispering Pines Trailhead, across the parking area from where you began the hike.

Nearby Attractions

Pickle Springs Natural Area is a must-see location, especially if you enjoy unusual geological formations (573-290-5730; nature.mdc .mo.gov/discover-nature/places/pickle-springs). It's a 12-mile drive from Hawn State Park.

Directions

From the junction of MO 32 and Washington Street/MO D in Farmington, travel east on MO 32 9.5 miles, then turn right (east) on MO 144 East and drive 3.0 miles. Turn left onto Park Drive and go 1.1 miles before veering right (south) to the Whispering Pines and Pickle Creek Trailheads and parking area.

Springfield Conservation Nature Center Loop

SCENERY: ★ ★ ★ ★
TRAIL CONDITION: ★ ★ ★ ★ ★
CHILDREN: ★ ★ ★ ★ ★
DIFFICULTY: ★ ★
SOLITUDE: ★ ★

THIS BOARDWALK CROSSES AN INLET OF LAKE SPRINGFIELD.

GPS TRAILHEAD COORDINATES: N37° 07.700' W93° 14.355'

DISTANCE AND CONFIGURATION: 2.5-mile figure eight

HIKING TIME: 1.5 hours

HIGHLIGHTS: Variety of natural environments, from savanna to deep hardwood forests located in an urban setting

ELEVATION: 1,287' at trailhead, 1,290' at highest point, 1,180' at lowest point

ACCESS: March–October: Daily, 8 a.m.–8 p.m.; November–February: Daily, 8 a.m.–6 p.m.; closed January 1, Thanksgiving, and December 25; no fees or permits required

MAPS: USGS *Galloway* and *Ozark*

FACILITIES: Restrooms and visitor center

WHEELCHAIR ACCESS: Access available on paved routes

COMMENTS: No pets allowed. Several short loop trail options are possible, so you can follow the described route or customize for your needs. Portions of this trail can be viewed via Street View on Google Earth. Enter the trailhead coordinates in the search box and preview parts of the trail before you go. Running is limited to posted hours.

CONTACTS: Springfield Conservation Nature Center, 417-888-4237, nature.mdc.mo.gov /discover-nature/places/springfield-cnc

Overview

This is a beautiful oasis of nature at the unlikely intersection of two major highways within the City of Springfield. The Springfield Conservation Nature Center has something for everyone. Trail runners, children, and those needing wheelchair access will find a path to their liking and opportunities to observe plants and animals in their natural setting.

This hike combines parts of the Savanna Ridge, Long, Fox Bluff, and Boardwalk Trails. All trails are well marked, and a map is available at the kiosk.

Route Details

You'll find the trailhead northeast of the nature center next to bus parking. Begin by heading northeast on the paved Savanna Ridge Trail that skirts the highway but has some great mixed hardwoods and occasional benches for breaks. You'll come pretty quickly to an intersection and stay to the left, passing through split rail fences and a quick view of the highway, but this doesn't last long.

At 0.1 mile, you'll arrive at the Long Trail junction. Turn left (northeast), leading off the paved route onto crushed gravel. The highway will be on your left as you circle down the hillside. Depending on the season, you may see wildflowers and blackberries in this savanna environment. The highway noise lessens as you reenter the woods at 0.2 mile and begin walking along a crosstie retaining wall through a boggy area.

At close to 0.5 mile, you'll pass through a little cedar grove, still on the Long Trail, and then come to a boardwalk, allowing access to some boggy areas. The trail comes alongside Galloway Creek.

You'll come to a bridge that crosses the small stream you've been walking next to and then a bridge over a tip of Lake Springfield before entering a savanna area. If you're walking in the early morning, you'll probably see deer in the surrounding vegetation.

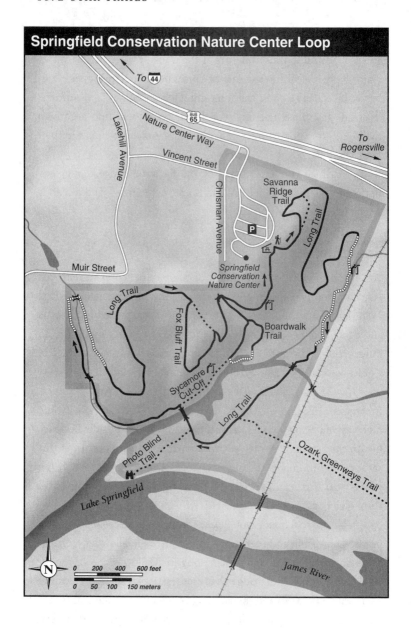

Springfield Conservation Nature Center Loop

To 44

Lakehill Avenue

Nature Center Way

BUS 65

Vincent Street

To Rogersville

Chrisman Avenue

Savanna Ridge Trail

Long Trail

P

Muir Street

Springfield Conservation Nature Center

Long Trail

Long Trail

Fox Bluff Trail

Boardwalk Trail

Sycamore Cut-Off

Long Trail

Photo Blind Trail

Ozark Greenways Trail

Lake Springfield

N

0   200   400   600 feet
0   50   100   150 meters

James River

At 0.8 mile, come to a sign that says To Greenways Trail. Do not take the Greenways route; continue straight on the Long Trail.

At about 1.0 mile, you come to another bridge back across the arm of Lake Springfield. Then turn left (west) and continue on the Long Trail. To the right is Sycamore Cut-Off, a shortcut you don't want to take. Walking Long Trail with the lake on your left, you'll feel like you're well out into the woods here. This is a nice walk with rock formations along the hillside on the right. Before long, veer right and start uphill slightly, following a stone path alongside an intermittent stream.

You'll pass a spring next to the trail that flows into the stream at 1.1 miles. The water is clear, but a sign reminds you that it's not for drinking. The highway noise is only a distant hum now.

The trail sweeps to the right and follows a long boardwalk with natural prairie areas that will be covered in wildflowers during spring and summer. The trail eventually leaves the boardwalk and heads back into the woods at a slight climb. As the hill tops out, there is a well-placed bench for a break.

At just after 1.6 miles, you'll come to a couple of spur trails to the service center and a residential road, but continue straight on the Long Trail.

At 1.8 miles, you'll turn right onto the Fox Bluff Trail, then come to an overlook and bench looking down the hillside. At close

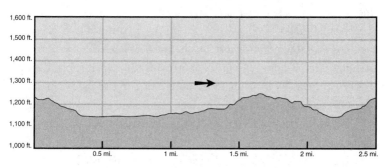

TAKING IN THE VIEW FROM THE BOARDWALK TRAIL OVERLOOK

to 1.9 miles, you'll come to a junction and turn right to continue on the Fox Bluff Trail. Left would take you back to the Long Trail. A sign indicates the nature center is 1.0 mile away.

At 2.0 miles, you'll take a right on the Boardwalk Trail. You'll definitely want to do this short loop before heading back toward the nature center. Follow the trail about 50 yards to where it splits, then turn right to follow the loop. At 2.2 miles, you come to the Sycamore Cut-Off, the other end of the shortcut you passed earlier. Turn left and follow the boardwalk across the edge of the arm of Lake Springfield and then back onto a paved trail. This little Boardwalk Trail would be great fun for kids and a good chance to spot wildlife.

Pretty quickly, the trail comes back to where you started this short loop. Turn right and follow the Boardwalk Trail toward the nature center. You'll pass a wooden overlook that places you up in the tree canopy. After enjoying the view, continue uphill to the nature center and trailhead to complete this 2.5-mile hike.

Nearby Attractions

Lake Springfield Park offers fishing, kayaks and canoes, and nature trails (417-891-1550; parkboard.org/1216/Lake-Springfield-Park-Boathouse-Marina).

Walnut Street Inn provides a relaxing atmosphere and elegant breakfasts. It's located in downtown historical Springfield and within walking distance of the Juanita K. Hammons Hall for the Performing Arts, Missouri State University, convention center, and a variety of restaurants. Best of all, it's only a 20-minute drive to the Springfield Conservation Nature Center (417-864-6346 or 800-593-6346; walnutstreetinn.com).

Directions

From I-44 in Springfield, drive east on US 60/James River Freeway, and take the Republic Road exit toward US 65 Business/Glenstone Avenue. Drive south 0.4 mile and use the middle lane to turn left onto East Republic Street (signs for US 65 Business/Evangel University/Glenstone Avenue). Turn right onto South Nature Center Way and drive 1.0 mile to the entrance of the Springfield Conservation Nature Center.

From Rogersville, drive west on US 60/James River Freeway, and take the US 65 Business exit toward Glenstone Avenue/Republic Road. Turn left onto South Glenstone Avenue and drive 0.1 mile. Turn left onto South Nature Center Way and drive 1.0 mile to the entrance of the Springfield Conservation Nature Center.

Clifty Creek Natural Area Loop

SCENERY: ★ ★ ★ ★ ★
TRAIL CONDITION: ★ ★ ★ ★ ★
CHILDREN: ★ ★ ★ ★ ★
DIFFICULTY: ★ ★ ★
SOLITUDE: ★ ★ ★

THE NATURAL ARCH OVER LITTLE CLIFTY CREEK

GPS TRAILHEAD COORDINATES: N38° 01.839' W91° 58.908'

DISTANCE AND CONFIGURATION: 2.5-mile loop

HIKING TIME: 2 hours

HIGHLIGHTS: Natural arch spans 40 feet across a small stream as it enters Clifty Creek. Visit dry glades and a lush Ozark stream environment that supports a wide variety of plant life.

ELEVATION: 878' at trailhead, 878' at highest point, 678' at lowest point

ACCESS: Daily, 4 a.m.–10 p.m.; no fees or permits required

MAPS: USGS *Nagogami Lodge;* may be available at trailhead kiosk

FACILITIES: None

WHEELCHAIR ACCESS: No

COMMENTS: Leashed pets are allowed. Hunting and fishing are permitted with appropriate licenses. Be prepared for two wet creek crossings.

CONTACTS: Missouri Department of Conservation, Central Regional Office, 573-815-7900, nature.mdc.mo.gov/discover-nature/places/clifty-creek

Overview

Clifty Creek contains a diverse collection of plants and animals. It also includes a natural arch, an iconic geological formation. The creek's name derives from the high cliffs in the area: local usage of the word *clift* became *clifty* to describe the creek. This trail is a pleasure every step of the way. The trail is well designed and constructed, taking you on a trip down into the Clifty Creek hollow and next to the arch, where erosion is still shaping the bluffs today.

Route Details

From the trailhead, walk about 400 feet to a junction and then turn right (north) to begin the loop. Enjoy the deep Clifty Creek hollow on your left and the surrounding scenic and well-managed forest. The trail trends downward to a switchback and split rail fence to keep you from going over the edge of a bluff at 0.3 mile. This is a nice spot to get a view of Clifty Creek upstream. A sign explains efforts to restore glades in this area.

When you get to the creek level, you're traveling downstream with Clifty Creek on your left. Several drainages flow across the trail as you climb above the creek. When the trees are leafless, you'll have open views all along this ridge looking down on Clifty Creek Valley. Be careful as you move up on top of the ridge because the trail skirts steep drop-offs. You'll see lots of deep-green moss-covered boulders as you travel this hillside in a northeasterly direction.

At 1.0 mile, arrive at Clifty Creek and come face to face with the natural arch. The massive arch spans the confluence of Little Clifty Creek, where it decided to take a shortcut through this dolomite bluff sometime in the geological past. Cross the creek with caution, and turn back if water is high or swift. When you arrive at the base of the arch, walk underneath to appreciate its size.

Keep in mind that the rock above you weighs about 170 pounds per cubic foot. Though solid and standing in its present form for several human lifetimes, it was carved by the relentless force of water

Clifty Creek Natural Area Loop

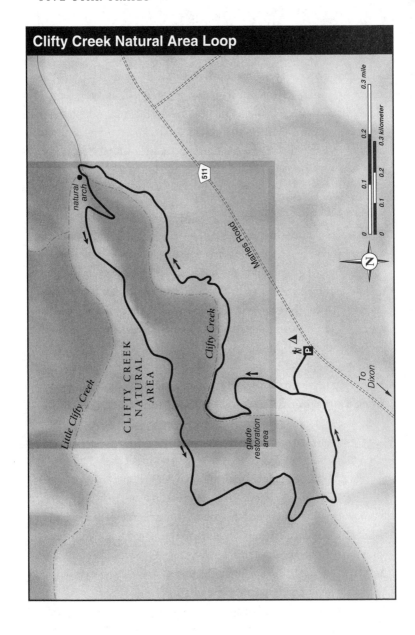

over time. Its form is still subject to change today. As impressive as the natural arch is due to its size and weight, you'll be even more awed by a quality that has *no* weight by the cubic foot: its *beauty*.

From the arch, follow the trail southwest, heading upstream with the bluff on your right. You'll switchback uphill and arrive on top of a ridge. At 1.5 miles, the ridge comes to its narrowest point, and you can see that it divides Clifty Creek to the south and Little Clifty Creek to the north.

Enjoy some easy ridge walking before passing through a small glade restoration area, where cedar trees are being cut to allow the natural grasses to become established. The trail begins a gradual descent to the crossing of Clifty Creek at 2.3 miles and then leads you back out of the hollow to the junction where you began this hike. Turn right and walk the short distance back to the trailhead.

Directions

From the town of Dixon, drive north on MO 28 3.9 miles to MO W. Turn right (east) on MO W and go approximately 3 miles. MO W ends, and the road changes from pavement to gravel to become County Road 511. Proceed east on the gravel road for about 0.7 mile and watch for the parking lot on the left (north) side of the road.

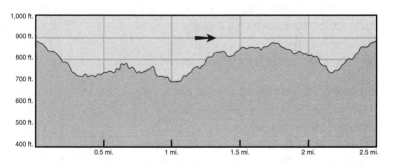

Maramec Spring Park Loop

CASCADES DOWNSTREAM FROM MARAMEC SPRING

GPS TRAILHEAD COORDINATES: N37° 57.260' W91° 32.064'

DISTANCE AND CONFIGURATION: 2.2-mile loop

HIKING TIME: 1.5 hours

HIGHLIGHTS: Maramec Spring and cascades, Maramec Branch, and ironworks historical structures

ELEVATION: 806' at trailhead, 806' at highest point, 770' at lowest point

ACCESS: Open 24/7; no fees or permits required

MAPS: USGS *Maramec Spring*

FACILITIES: Restrooms and water during the warmer seasons

WHEELCHAIR ACCESS: Portions of the paths are paved and wheelchair accessible.

COMMENTS: Leashed pets are allowed.

CONTACTS: Maramec Spring Park, 573-265-7387, maramecspringpark.com

Overview

Maramec Spring trails are great for families and history buffs. The fascinating history of Maramec Iron Works complements the spring's natural beauty. Portions of the paved paths take you through an out-door museum of the Maramec Iron Works. Thomas James, an Ohio businessman, began construction in 1826, and then in 1843 he sent his son William James to operate the ironworks.

The Civil War increased the demand for iron from the plant, in spite of the transportation challenges of this remote location. At its peak, the town was reported to have close to 500 residents. The Maramec Iron Works ceased operation in 1876.

A descendant of William James, Lucy Wortham James, estab-lished the James Foundation upon her death in 1938 to protect this area. She wrote the following: "As this is considered to be the most beautiful spot in Missouri, it is my great hope that you will arrange that it may ever be in private, considerate control, and ever open to the enjoyment of the people."

Route Details

Begin this hike at the parking lot for the Maramec Iron Works Museum next to Maramec Spring. Follow a sign pointing you to the right (south) to Maramec Spring. A series of wheelchair-accessible paved paths is in the area of the spring. You'll use both paved and dirt paths for this loop hike. Walk next to a cedar split rail fence and past a trail information box that might have brochures if you're visiting in season. During winter, you'll likely have the spring to yourself.

A sign at the Maramec Spring says its flow is 96.3 million gal-lons per day, making it the fifth-largest spring in Missouri. At 0.2 mile, you'll come to the actual spring, with a metal railing along the paved path. This spring, located at the base of a bluff, is subtle but beautiful. The entrance to an underwater cave is several feet below the surface. Divers have explored about 1 mile of this cave, and a video about the world below the surface may be viewed in the museum.

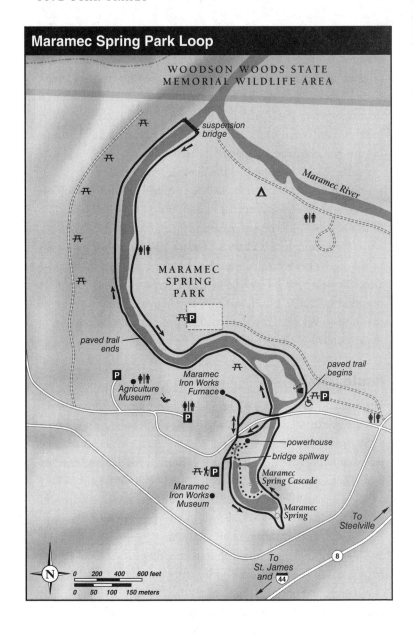

Maramec Spring Park Loop

WOODSON WOODS STATE
MEMORIAL WILDLIFE AREA

Maramec River

suspension
bridge

MARAMEC
SPRING
PARK

paved trail
ends

paved trail
begins

Maramec
Iron Works
Furnace

Agriculture
Museum

powerhouse

bridge spillway

Maramec
Spring Cascade

Maramec
Iron Works
Museum

Maramec
Spring

To
Steelville

To
St. James
and 44

8

N

0   200   400   600 feet

0   50   100   150 meters

The volume of water flowing out of this spring doesn't become evident until you view a cascade just down from the spring. Another demonstration of flow rate is on display at a bridged spillway downstream. This water will travel about 165 river miles to where the Maramec River empties into the Mississippi River.

After the cascade, you'll pass trout hatchery pools and may see workers feeding the growing trout a couple of times each day. You'll see rotating screens that separate the trout by size. Continue to a small footbridge. Steps lead up to a picnic area and trout fishing area beyond.

You'll pass a powerhouse that was used in the 1920s to generate electricity for the dairy farm and ice plant. At 0.5 mile, you'll pass under a bridge and arrive at a junction, where you'll take a right and begin walking through what can only be called an outdoor museum. Ironworks artifacts are all around the path and include interpretative signs. You'll visit the Maramec Iron Works Furnace after your return from Maramec Spring Branch.

The flow from Maramec Spring widens into a creek channel where fly fishermen enjoy their pursuit of trout, visible just below the clear currents. You're walking with the Maramec Branch flowing downstream on your right. You'll pass a stairwell that leads to a recreational area higher above the creek, but continue straight downstream.

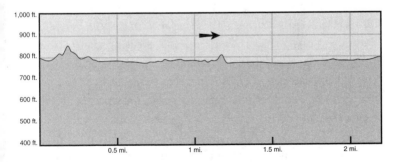

THE POWERHOUSE, ONE OF MANY HISTORICAL STRUCTURES AT MARAMEC SPRING

Where the paved path ends, a dirt trail begins. Continue down the creek and cross a suspension bridge at 1.3 miles. After crossing the bridge, turn right (southwest). Now you're walking back upstream on Maramec Branch with the stream down on your right. There are several little walk-out spots for fishing, but they're also good for getting views up and down this beautiful creek. You'll pass restrooms on your left.

You'll come alongside a parking area on your left at 1.7 miles. The Maramec Branch widens, and the path returns to pavement at 1.9 miles. You'll see a row of interpretive signs. This route returns to the ironworks "outdoor museum." This is a great place to explore iron and stone structures, some of which date back to the 1820s. Take a short out-and-back to the massive casting arch of the Maramec Iron Works Furnace. Return to your route leading back under the road and along a boardwalk to the Maramec Iron Works Museum parking lot. You've logged about 2.2 miles at this point, but you might want to explore this fascinating area some more before you go.

While hiking the Maramec Spring in winter is a pleasure, you'll miss out on visiting the Maramec Iron Works Museum, which closes at the end of October and reopens in the spring. Winter is my favorite because of the steam you're likely to see rising above the spring and cascades. If you're an early-morning hiker, you might see some frost flowers next to the creek.

You may feel a tinge of sadness as you drive away from Maramec Spring. Pause and be thankful that William James's granddaughter, Lucy Wortham James, chose to protect this area for us to see today.

Directions

From the town of St. James on I-44, follow the scenic MO 8 to the southeast 8.0 miles, and then turn left onto Maramec Spring Drive. Drive 0.2 mile to the parking lot for the Maramec Iron Works Museum.

GRANNY HENDERSON'S CABIN ON THE HEMMED-IN HOLLOW TRAIL *(See Hike 14, page 93.)*

Appendix A:
Area Outdoor Retailers

Because hiking is a major activity in the Ozarks, resources for gear and other essentials abound in Arkansas and Missouri. Below are several suppliers.

ALPINE SHOP
888-DISCVRY (347-2879)
alpineshop.com

440 N Kirkwood Road
Kirkwood, MO 63122
314-962-7715

1616 Clarkson Road
Chesterfield, MO 63017
636-532-7499

1102 E Broadway (at Hitt)
Columbia, MO 65201
573-817-2955

LEWIS & CLARK OUTFITTERS
gooutandplay.com

4915 S Thompson St.
Springdale, AR 72764
479-756-1344

2530 Pinnacle Hills Pkwy.
Rogers, AR 72758
479-845-1344

OZARK OUTDOOR SUPPLY
5514 Kavanaugh Blvd.
Little Rock, AR 72207
501-664-4832 or 877-OZARK-30
ozarkoutdoor.com

PACK RAT OUTDOOR CENTER
209 W Sunbridge Drive
Fayetteville, AR 72703
479-521-6340
packratoc.com

REI
rei.com

1703 S Brentwood Blvd.
Saint Louis, MO 63144
314-918-1004

6281 W 135th St.
Kansas City, MO 66223
913-402-1938

THE WOODSMAN COMPANY
5111 Rogers Ave., Central Mall
Fort Smith, AR
479-452-3559
facebook.com/TheWoodsmanCompany

Appendix B: Maps

In addition to the locations listed in Appendix A, here are some contacts for acquiring maps of the areas covered in this trail guide.

OZARK HIGHLANDS TRAIL ASSOCIATION
ozarkhighlandstrail.com

OZARK TRAIL ASSOCIATION
573-436-0540
ozarktrail.com

TIM ERNST, CLOUDLAND PUBLISHING
870-861-5536
Book/print order line: 800-838-HIKE (4453)
timernst.com

U.S. GEOLOGICAL SURVEY
888-275-8747
usgs.gov

Appendix C:
Hiking Clubs

A number of hiking clubs are found in the Ozarks of Arkansas and Missouri. This is only a partial list showing some of the more active hiking clubs in the Ozarks.

FRIENDS OF THE OUACHITA TRAIL (FoOT)
friendsot.org

HIKING THE OZARKS
hikingtheozarks.com

MISSOURI CHAPTER OF THE SIERRA CLUB
800-628-5333 or 314-644-1011
missouri2.sierraclub.org

OUACHITA MOUNTAIN HIKERS
omhikers.net

OZARK HIGHLANDS TRAIL ASSOCIATION
ozarkhighlandstrail.com

OZARK SOCIETY
ozarksociety.net

OZARK TRAIL ASSOCIATION
573-436-0540
ozarktrail.com

TAKAHIK RIVER VALLEY HIKERS
takahik.com

TRAILBLAZERS HIKING CLUB
thcfs.com

LONG CREEK FALLS IN THE HERCULES GLADES WILDERNESS
(See Hike 26, page 162.)

Index

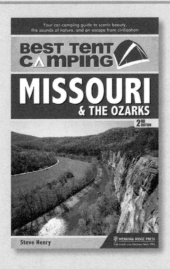

About the Author

GROWING UP IN ARKANSAS, JIM WARNOCK enjoyed day hikes with his parents on family camping trips and in the woods behind his home. He found hiking to be essential to his physical health and in maintaining relationships with family and friends.

photographed by Bob Cable

His love of hiking led him to like-minded friends who have hiked Arkansas, Missouri, New Mexico, and Colorado and have made repeated trips into the Grand Canyon of Arizona. He thru-hiked the Ozark Highlands Trail in January 2014 and completed the John Muir Trail in the summer of 2016.

While he's come to love the long and legendary trails, he relishes the joys of day hikes and finds that they provide endless discovery and pleasure with limited travel time and expense. As an educator and school principal, he has unique insight into the needs of young hikers. In his book, you'll find trails for the experienced outdoors enthusiast seeking a challenge as well as for the novice or young hiker who benefits from shorter hikes that hold interest and provide new learning.

Jim was designated as a National Distinguished School Principal in 2006 and has served as president of the Arkansas Association of Educational Administrators. He currently serves as a board member of the Ozark Highlands Trail Association (OHTA) and maintains memberships in both the OHTA in Arkansas and the Ozark Trail Association in Missouri.

Jim has written numerous articles on hiking and travel for *Do South Magazine* and *Entertainment Fort Smith*. He has also written for state and national educational leadership publications and has served as an editorial advisor for *Principal Magazine*.

When not hiking and writing about trails, Jim might be found maintaining his adopted 4-mile section of the Ozark Highlands Trail from Jack Creek to Dockery Gap. He enjoys photography, blogging, drumming, and daily hikes on the Lake Alma Trail with his black Lab, Hiker-dog. You can follow their current outdoor travels at ozarkmountainhiker.com.

DEAR CUSTOMERS AND FRIENDS,

SUPPORTING YOUR INTEREST IN OUTDOOR ADVENTURE, travel, and an active lifestyle is central to our operations, from the authors we choose to the locations we detail to the way we design our books. Menasha Ridge Press was incorporated in 198 by a group of veteran outdoorsmen and professional outfitters. For many years now, we've specialized in creating books that benefit the outdoors enthusiast.

Almost immediately, Menasha Ridge Press earned a reputation for revolutionizing outdoors- and travel-guidebook publishing. For such activities as canoeing, kayaking, hiking, backpacking and mountain biking, we established new standards of quality that transformed the whole genre, resulting in outdoor-recreation guides of great sophistication and solid content. Menasha Ridge Press continues to be outdoor publishing's greatest innovator.

The folks at Menasha Ridge Press are as at home on a whitewater river or mountain trail as they are editing a manuscript. The books we build for you are the best they can be, because we're responding to your needs. Plus, we use and depend on them ourselves.

We look forward to seeing you on the river or the trail. If you'd like to contact us directly, visit us at menasharidge.com. We thank you for your interest in our books and the natural world around us all.

SAFE TRAVELS,

Bob Sehlinger

BOB SEHLINGER
PUBLISHER